Acclaim
Diary of a Country Therapist

"My wish is that everyone would read this book at least once and therapists at least twice. First, read it just to enjoy the wisdom and the lovely writing. And for therapists, read it again to integrate this profound wisdom into your work. It's a rare therapist who is such a fine writer. Perhaps even more rare is the combination of depth and humility that sing along in this lyrical book."

—Jean Baker Miller, MD
Director, Jean Baker Miller Training Institute,
Stone Center, Wellesley College

"This book is a page-turner! I wanted to find out more and more about the life and work of this sensitive, insightful, engaged, and complex 'country therapist.' I never tired of finding out what would happen next—as in effective psychotherapy. I highly recommend this book to therapists at all stages of development. It will reflect yourself and your life back to you."

—Polly Young-Eisendrath, PhD
Author of *Women & Desire:*
Beyond Wanting to Be Wanted
and *The Resilient Spirit*

"Marcia Hill is a brilliant psychotherapist and a first-rate writer. She is also a master conjurer. In her adroit hands, her therapy office is a mysterious universe, teeming with ghosts and demons, waifs and heroes. In her world, it is impossible to know who—the therapist or the client—is more wounded or healed, who more transformed by the process of therapy. The only certainty is that those lucky enough to enter Hill's realm are privy to the subtle secrets of everyday magic. Hill also writes exquisitely about the world beyond the therapy office. Her depictions of rural Vermont, its seasons and its solitude, are as immediate as an Imogene Cunningham photograph, as timeless as a May Sarton prose poem. This is a luminous, landmark volume. I highly recommend it for anyone fascinated by the paradoxes of human connection."

—Marny Hall, PhD, LCSW
Author of *The Lesbian Love Companion*

"Marcia Hill eased my loneliness with her book. It was as if she had crawled inside my head and found my inner therapist's self, not the one that talks to other people, but the one that holds dear the thoughts, joys, and pains of my clients—and myself. Her beautiful prose is yet another reason to savor her book. If I ran a graduate program, I'd require this book for all new therapists. Hill writes about being a therapist who helps people grow, heal, and sometimes change who they are. We don't train new therapists about this and we should. I would also give her book to all the experienced therapists I know, because we all need good company."

—G. Dorsey Green, PhD
Adjunct Clinical Instructor,
University of Washington;
Co-author of *Lesbian Couples*
and *The Lesbian Parenting Book*

Diary of a Country Therapist

THE HAWORTH PRESS
New, Recent, and Forthcoming Titles of Related Interest

Diary of a Country Therapist

Marcia Hill

The Haworth Press®
New York • London • Oxford

The Haworth Press, Inc., 10 Alice Street, Binghamton, NY 13904-1580.

A version of "The Truth About Relationships" was first published in 2002 in *In the Family,* 7 (4), p. 27. "Counting My Blessings" is adapted from "Changes: The Personal Consequences of the Practice of Psychotherapy," previously published in 1997 in *More Than a Mirror,* Marcia Hill (Ed.), by The Haworth Press, Inc.

PUBLISHER'S NOTE
Identities and circumstances of individuals discussed in this book have been changed to protect confidentiality.

Cover design by Marylouise Doyle.

Library of Congress Cataloging-in-Publication Data

Hill, Marcia.
    Diary of a country therapist / Marcia Hill.
        p. cm.
    Includes bibliographical references.
    ISBN 0-7890-2115-3 (case : alk. paper)—ISBN 0-7890-2116-1 (soft : alk. paper)
    1. Hill, Marcia—Diaries. 2. Psychotherapists—Vermont—Diaries. 3. Psychotherapy—Practice—Psychological aspects. 4. Psychotherapists—Psychology. I. Title.
RC438.6.H55A3 2004
616.89'14'092—dc22
                                                                                    2003021898

CONTENTS

෨ 1999 ෬

෨ 2000 ෬

෨ CONCLUSION ෬

ABOUT THE AUTHOR

Marcia Hill, EdD, is a psychologist in private practice who has spent over twenty-five years practicing psychotherapy. She is a former co-editor of the journal *Women & Therapy* and a member and past Chair of the Feminist Therapy Institute. In addition to therapy, Dr. Hill does occasional teaching, writing, and consulting in the areas of feminist therapy theory and practice. She has edited or co-edited nine Haworth books: *Classism and Feminist Therapy: Counting Costs* (1996); *Couples Therapy: Feminist Perspectives* (1996); *More Than a Mirror: How Clients Influence Therapists' Lives* (1997); *Children's Rights, Therapists' Responsibilities: Feminist Commentaries* (1997); *Breaking the Rules: Women in Prison and Feminist Therapy* (1998); *Feminist Therapy As a Political Act* (1998); *Learning from Our Mistakes: Difficulties and Failures in Feminist Therapy* (1998); *Beyond the Rule Book: Moral Issues and Dilemmas in the Practice of Psychotherapy* (1999); and *For Love or Money: The Fee in Feminist Therapy* (1999).

ଧ *INTRODUCTION* ଓ

But First, a Word
from My Sponsors

I wonder if anyone ever just sits down and writes a book all alone? We're a social species; minding one another's business is our nature. I'm a psychologist, and by dint of my profession I have learned that other people are my best resource when I feel stuck or uncertain and they are my best comfort when I have the writing willies.

Some people encouraged me at critical junctures, times when I had stopped writing or doubted that it was worth going forward. I count Michele Clark, Deb Crespin, Marny Hall, Joann Hinz, and Barbara Watkins (who also suggested the title for this book) among them. Karen Grace and Shoshanna Shelley were my steadfast fan club of two who cheered me on and helped me obsess about confidentiality, even when we were all somewhat muddled with food and wine. Kristin Glaser jump-started this project's beginnings. My "book midwife," Caroline Pincus, steered me through the mysteries of writing a proposal and approaching publishers. When I was worried about how to protect client privacy, Peter Kramer generously responded to my plea for guidance. I have tried to follow his advice to disguise client material to the point of fiction.

A series of readers helped me get through my initial reaction of "Yikes, someone else might actually read this!" and offered thoughtful suggestions for improvement. Thanks to Gail Anderson, Dorsey Green, Jamie Miller, Pat Lyon-Surrey, and Penny Sablove. The book you hold is much enriched because of them.

Paul Hanlon, Judy Harden, and Esther Rothblum were my faithful supporters throughout the writing. Believe me, it was a long labor, and not just anyone has what it takes to stay the course with a twitchy author. I'm grateful.

Finally, to those clients past and future who have shared their lives with me, you are in many ways the true authors of this book. Congratulations on its publication. And thank you for making me the person I am today.

Welcome

This is a chronicle of more than ten years as a psychotherapist. Can you remember who you were ten years ago? At the start of this writing, I was forty and had been a therapist for fifteen years. I had never had a challenge to my health; I had experienced no primary losses. My work life felt secure. I can claim none of that now. Ten years is a lifetime when the givens of your life change. But those are only the story lines. Can you recall the way you looked at life, what you felt was possible, what you thought mattered? If this time has brought me some complexity of understanding and depth of perspective, how limited still will that look to me in another ten years? In twenty? Ten years is no time at all in the development of a spirit.

Because I'm a therapist, my life story is intertwined with those of many others, people who have inspired the emotions and ideas behind these essays, people whose pain and courage and grace have become part of my own life's fabric. I cannot tell my story without telling theirs. Their privacy is my first commitment, however, and so I have invented more than I have borrowed when describing any person. Often I have combined people, or started with the feeling of an event and created a narrative based only loosely, if at all, on the incident that inspired it. My goal has been to tell the truth, not necessarily the reality. Further, the human journey is not only individual, but is also one of shared themes. The reader who glimpses someone familiar is, in fact, recognizing the commonalities in human experience.

The task of therapy is to birth change, but my clients are not the only ones who have changed. You will find here my own evolution as a therapist and as a person. You will find also the effects of market forces on the field of psychotherapy: a picture of this country making one of the last efforts among developed nations to use capitalism to address health care. It has been an expensive experiment in more ways than financial.

Aloneness is part of the human condition; it drives our need for one another. We can never fully understand another person, never really get inside another's life. I know: in my work I have had more opportunity to try than most. But it's human nature to hunger for connection. We talk incessantly to one another, we invent psychotherapy, we write biographies and memoirs. We look into our lovers' eyes, ask our friends questions, imagine what goes on in other people's houses. And we tell our own secrets and sorrows and triumphs to those we trust. Separation is our birthright, yet we spend our whole lives looking for company. Here, then, is one therapist's experience, a decade of one woman's life. My hope for these pages is that in them we can find one another.

ಜಿ *1989* ಛ

Putting the Heart to Work

What a strange line of work this is, where the ability to feel is such a primary tool. Who would think that one's heart could be harnessed and used intentionally as a resource? It's such a paradox. My feeling response is what it is, and cannot be commanded or faked. Yet it is not a matter of giving in to emotion but one of using feeling purposefully, like a scalpel. It's an experience of simultaneous yielding and restraint. The job of the professional empath is like that of the artist or poet—to take raw experience, direct emotional response, and somehow make it a vehicle for change and enlightenment.

I met today with a woman who is very controlled, rigidly closed off from her vulnerability, and—not surprisingly—depressed. She sat across from me like some beautiful carving, perfectly put together, untouchable. She talked about herself as a young girl, describing one of those insidiously destructive childhoods in which "nothing bad happened." She was not hit or molested or tortured in any of the various overt ways that adults use to express their pain on the bodies and spirits of the children they love. She was also not spoken to in kindness, not shown affection, not responded to with warmth or pride or welcome. She described an incident in fifth grade that occurred as she was working on a project with a classmate. The teacher came over to look at the work the two had done, and commented on how well done it was. As I listened, somewhere in my chest there was a familiar sensation of pain; I felt a slight urge to cry. I reached internally for the information that my body already knew. The woman who sat across from me is fifty-two, and has carried this memory like a treasure for over forty years. What did it mean for her to live a childhood so emotionally impoverished that she had held on to a single kind word from a teacher to sustain her? I said that to her, letting my voice and body express what I knew of her pain, and saw her begin to allow herself a fuller response to that memory. She would not let herself really cry yet, but her eyes filled with tears and her mouth trembled. She told me more. In the course of the hour we did this several times. At the end of the time she was visibly softer. My throat aches from the weeping that she hasn't done. I sigh, relax my body, let it go.

With someone else today, I shared grief at her mother's death; with another woman, I joined her rage at being sexually harassed in the workplace. I kept another client company as she struggled with massive anxiety that made it difficult for her to speak at all. What does it do to me to have this level of feeling pouring through me day after day? I discussed this with my dentist the other day, as best I could with his hands in my mouth. We compared notes on our jobs. I asked him how it was to be constantly touching people who were nervous. He said that he was used to it and hardly noticed. Then, more thoughtfully, he added, "That doesn't mean it's not affecting my stomach lining, I suppose."

I'm used to strong feelings. Empathy comes easily, and with rare exceptions I can let my emotional response leave the room with the client at the end of the hour. Still, I imagine that sorrow is gradually making a dent in my heart. Rage and terror and the wild grief of loss walk through my body's home like cats, leaving muddy footprints on the floor and scratching the furniture. But in spite of that, how could I possibly do anything else for work?

Let Me Go!

Not quite two weeks before I leave on vacation, a former client calls me for an appointment. She doesn't sound good on the phone, and I can hear the tears behind her words. I meet with her a couple of days later. She is very depressed, crying much of the time, can't go to work or do much more than basic care for her small child. We strategize: a call to her physician to see about raising the dosage of the antidepressant she is already taking, some ideas about ways to get through the rough spell, the nonmedical things that tend to help depression. I'm worried about her.

It's now a week and a half before my vacation. Another client, at his regular appointment, is descending into his own personal hell of anxiety. He's had times like this before, but not in a long while. Why now? He knows what to do to help anxiety, and those things do help, but not enough to make the beast release its grip on him. I keep him company and try to figure out where it came from, but we don't get far. He's holding his own, though, and we both hope that it will pass, one of those things that comes and goes for its own reasons.

A week before my vacation. I meet again with the depressed woman. Not good. She's no longer having suicidal thoughts, but otherwise her distress is just as bad. This is her second depressive episode, but the first wasn't nearly this tough. I am able to reassure her a bit, but the truth is that she will have to endure feeling miserable for a while. We figure out resources for help with her toddler, and we plan another meeting for before I leave.

Three days before. There's a call on my machine from this same woman. She sounds awful. I call her back; by then, she's doing a bit better, but it's really just a matter of whether she's feeling bad or worse at any given moment. I have another meeting with the young man who is anxious. If anything, he's suffering more. He can't stop hyperventilating, can't get enough past his terror that he's having a heart attack to do anything approaching therapy. He's spiraling away, past the point where my words can reach him. With my encouragement, he calls his doctor from my office and asks if he can get some antianxiety medication. They give him an appointment for first thing the next morning.

Two days before. I hear from a couple I saw some months ago. They want an appointment as soon as possible; they're in bad trouble, they say. I talk with them, determine that it's not an emergency, and schedule them for as soon as I get back. I also get a call from a woman who finished her therapy about a month ago. She was unexpectedly fired from her job a few days ago, then last night her boyfriend of four years ended their relationship. I squeeze her in for the next day. I check in with the client who has the awful anxiety; he got some medication, took it, fell into an exhausted sleep, and is at least a bit back from the brink. Now there's a chance that talking can help.

That night, at 9:00 p.m., I get a call at home from a client who is in a relationship with an alcoholic and who also abuses alcohol herself. We've been talking about her drinking for some time. She tells me that she finally wants to do something about it and would like to go into a treatment program. Tonight. I offer my blessing but luckily need not do much more; it turns out that she has already called the treatment program and has arranged for a friend to drive her there. Interesting timing.

The day before. There's a call on my answering machine from a client who has a sexual abuse history, although she has been doing fine lately. She wants to know who my backup is for when I'm away. By now I'm completely overreactive to potential crises, of course, and give her the information, but then ask why she needs to know. She's okay, she says, just wants the reassurance that someone is there. This is someone that I've seen for a while; she is well aware that I leave backup information on my answering machine. Something else is going on here. I make a mental note to talk with her about it when I see her next. I meet with the woman who has lost both her job and her boy-friend. She's hanging in there but is glad for the chance to check in with me about it. I am too.

It's the day I plan to leave. I meet with the woman who is de-pressed. We review and refine her plans for keeping her head above water. She'll be all right, I think, but I ache when she leaves my office. I wish the timing of my vacation didn't mean she was left without my support just now. The therapist I have for backup is experienced and very competent and I have no qualms about her ability to handle whatever comes along. But for my clients, I know, it just isn't the same. I meet also with the man who is anxious. He's still uncomfort-able but not quite as bad as when I last saw him. He mentions a phone call from his father that occurred just before this horrible episode. His father wanted him to know that he'd just had the family pet, the dog my client grew up with, the animal who was his only reliable source of loving approval, euthanized. This dog was not even ill, although she was old. My client, of course, had not been warned or consulted. This is someone who has wanted nothing more in his life than his father's approval and love; what he got on the phone was a cold pointed hos-tility, an arrow aimed surgically at where it would hurt most. No wonder this man had been having a meltdown. He had not put the two together before now. I don't feel great about going away just as he comes to this understanding, but I have some hope that knowing where his distress came from will make a difference. He asks me to tell him again that what his father did was in fact cruel. He has lived with this kind of treatment for so long that he is not sure.

Finally, midafternoon, I change the message on my answering ma-chine to say that I'm away and leave the office. Usually it's not this bad, but often the timing of my vacation is terrible for somebody. And some people seem to time their crises with my absence for any number of reasons: to prove to themselves that they really are alone, to let me know that they feel abandoned or angry that I am leaving, to express dependence. Some people are arranging for me to fail a test of love. If I truly cared for them, wouldn't I stay when they needed me? It's confusing for those people, I think. They can accurately feel their unmet needs as young children to come first with their parents, and thus with me. But they are also adults now and need to see my commitment to them balanced with my responsibility to myself.

For others, it's just bad luck. I have several hundred appointments a year, with several dozen people, and any week chosen at random has a reasonable chance of being a critical time for someone. I feel like the good mother who wishes to stay home with her ailing child. But this is my own life first. The airlines are right: put your own oxygen mask on first, then assist others.

Professional Loneliness

MARCH 16, 1989

I've joined the Feminist Therapy Institute (FTI) recently, and I have been enormously relieved to find colleagues who "speak my language." You would think that people in the same profession (psychotherapy) would all be able to talk shop with one another, and that if you found another therapist with whom you were reasonably compatible personally, that would do the trick. To some extent that's true. Any other therapist has some sense of the rewards and struggles of the job, shares some basic understanding of what therapy is all about. If someone has a similar theoretical stance, the match is even better. Still, the theoretical approaches to therapy are legion. To make the picture even more complex, the therapist's level of experience and personal style can make an enormous difference in how she or he understands the work.

As I write this, I realize that somehow just experience and theoretical orientation, even though they do help define the parameters that would point toward a match, don't really capture the essence of it. Skill, although related to experience, doesn't get earned simply with time. A number of other experienced therapists practice in town, but I would describe only a few as truly skilled. The other factor is that theoretical orientation, what therapists use to describe their work, is notoriously bad as a real indicator of what people are actually doing in their offices. We call ourselves this or that, and use a particular language to explain what we imagine we are doing to help our clients. In the meantime, with the reality of another human being in the chair across from us, we do what we've learned works, what meets our personal needs to nurture or feel wise (or whatever), what our unconscious mind (hopefully fully informed by paying close attention to previous therapy sessions!) comes up with at the moment.

The members of FTI are in some ways as varied as any other group of therapists: more and less skillful, with a range of theoretical perspectives, serving a variety of clientele. But all understand that emotional pain occurs in a social context. We don't need to explain to one another that gender—including the injuries of gender—is central to who a person is, or to how she or he approaches relationships, or to what options for change would even occur to him or her. We all know that what looks like anxiety or depression can just as easily be the effects of racism or homophobia. We agree implicitly that sexual trauma is a cultural phenomenon, not a personal one. Our goal with clients is not necessarily comfort with the status quo. To that end, we work hard to meet our clients on an equal footing in the ways that we can, to avoid the subtle arrogance and condescension that so often accompany the role of the helper. We give clients more information than other therapists. Knowledge is indeed power. We try not to act as if we know what's best for someone, working to stay honest about our assumptions and biases and to keep one another honest, too. We don't kid ourselves that therapy is value-free.

This is the heart of the feminist therapist's work. Next to this, our theories of change fade in importance. If I can share this way of operating, which shades and shapes every choice I make in my work, then I feel richly understood by my colleagues.

Therapy is very lonely work, which seems such an odd thing to say about a job that is based in relationship. The relationship is *for* the other person, though, and so while satisfying in many ways to the therapist, it is not nourishing in the way that a more mutual relationship (for example, a friendship) is. The therapist's responsibility to the other leaves her or him alone. It's a strange paradox that the intimacy of therapy is what, at least for me, seems to heighten that sense of isolation. How peculiar, when you think of it, to have an intense emotional encounter with a client, to do that intentionally, and then to step out of the room, go about one's business, and tell nobody. "How was your day?" "Oh, fine." Fine? More accurately: two fairly "normal" conversations about how people are doing in their lives; one discussion of family secrets; one exchange with a client about our relationship on a level of honesty that would give most people palpitations; one imagery session that was so unlike anything resembling normal conversation that an observer might well wonder about the *therapist's* contact with reality, let alone the client's; one hour's worth of anguished weeping; and one woman tormented in her effort to express some very disturbing feelings, hyperventilating and clutching the chair.

It's easy to see how much a feeling of real colleagueship can matter. This kind of day is not exactly something you blather about to anyone who is interested, even if considerations of confidentiality could be put aside, which they can't. I want to make it clear that the day I described is an average one, not at all one that I would carry with me as distressing or difficult. How can I continue to accompany people in this way if I do not feel at least somewhat accompanied myself?

The Gift of Transference

Difficult as it can be, I love working with the transference, with what Laura Brown calls the "symbolic relationship" between myself and the client. There's something so immediate, so alive, when the client brings childhood pain and need directly into the relationship with me. Then we're not just talking about how the client's parents hurt or failed him or her; we have more than the memories of being six years old, more than abstract information about how what was learned at six still affects his or her life today. Then we have, essentially, the actual six-year-old seeing his or her mother in the present. Then the anguish of the past and the not-yet-dared-for hope of some unarticulated possibility for the future collide in my office. The chance for change is so great, the moment so sacred, that I find myself shifting without thought into the best of who I am. My response from that self is accurate, powerful, and without ego.

One of my clients is a welder, a small wiry woman, tough and hidden. Her feelings are sophisticated, but her words are not; she says little and shows less. This week she was fumbling, with effort, toward some way to describe her feelings about me—meaning, of course, her feelings about her mother. We circled around the matter, uncertain, until there it was: out of a history of extreme neglect, from the hard lesson of there never being enough, came her expectation that certainly I would not have enough for her either. We stopped, absorbing the meaning of that. "We need to say something to that kid," I say. She nods, mutely: permission. So I go ahead, speaking to her child self's loss and neglect and suspiciousness and hope. She turns her chair away from me, weeping without sound, released.

This is the gift of transference: when the client expects from me what she learned to expect from her mother, then I have the opportunity to respond in the way that she needs but does not expect, the way that her mother could not. It's a way to honor that mother, I think, who would wish happiness for her daughter. The woman in front of me, given her experience of my understanding, will eventually come to expect responsiveness rather than neglect in her relationships.

It seems to me that much of the best work I do is more kinesthetic than verbal. If I enter into the experience of hurt empathetically, I know from inside what is needed to release the pain. I can tell how effective it's been by the echoed shift in myself. It's not exactly what they teach you in graduate school! Occasionally I wonder whatever possesses me to climb down into those dark achy places with people, over and over again. After all, it hurts me too. But it feels worth it for that moment of opening, of grace, like lifting off into flight.

The Feminist Gets Nervous

JULY 15, 1989

Recently I gave a presentation on feminist therapy at a local college. The audience was counseling students, predominately women. Their reaction to even basic feminist principles was discomfort, expressed by arguing about the ideas I described. They offered examples of "reverse discrimination" and of women misusing power with other women. One woman announced that while she agreed with the ideas presented, she was uncomfortable with the word *feminist*. A number of students kept arguing that *feminist* was an inappropriate descriptor, since issues of power were not necessarily associated with gender. I felt as if I were espousing something out of date and slightly embarrassing, like a bouffant hairdo. The level of naïveté was astonishing. A couple of students thought that feminist therapy was no different from what all therapists do. (They should talk with any one of my clients who has been to a nonfeminist therapist.)

In sum, they protest too much. What's so scary about the word *feminist?* About the concept of oppression based on gender? At times I resorted to analogies based on racial oppression—no one seemed to have any trouble with that. This country hasn't become a whole lot less racist, but at least we don't appear to be confused about the concept. Among liberals, anyway, there's agreement that racism is wrong. Yet admitting that sexism *exists* makes people nervous. I don't get it.

Last week I attended a meeting of a group of women who were discussing possible responses to the Supreme Court's *Webster* decision (restricting abortion rights). These, presumably, are the area's conscious women, but there was a clear concern that we not appear too radical, that we look like good girls who are happy to work within the (male-defined) system, who aren't about to threaten the order of things. A group of wealthy, white heterosexual men have made enforced pregnancy legal in some states and we don't feel the need to challenge the order of things?

Robin Morgan once said that becoming conscious (as a feminist) was the hardest thing she had ever done. I know what she's talking about; I spent years feeling enraged, despairing, and alienated. These were the dues of consciousness. Yet becoming conscious has also been one of the most joyful and powerful experiences I have known. Feminism is fundamental to my way of understanding the world. It makes me feel crazy when I see that these counselors-to-be do not *admit* to, let alone understand, the basic functioning of discrimination along the lines of gender, particularly when I know they would readily agree that racial discrimination is real. The Supreme Court decision is distressing because this decision is not just a matter of abortion rights. It signals the leaching out of conscience, of ethics, from the culture in general. It is one of many signs that indicates society's increasing fear of difference. I am a woman and an individual whose life is not mainstream. And I am frightened.

Be Careful What You Ask For

My last meeting of the board of directors (for a community women's organization) was this month. I don't remember the timing, but it's safe to say that it's been more than ten years; time to move on. This is something I helped to start. I've hired every person that's worked there since the beginning. My language has shaped the majority of the policies. I don't exactly feel ownership, but I do feel my print on the organization. It's not easy to let it go.

How will they manage without me? This sounds embarrassingly arrogant, but there it is. We (yes, I know) need to hire a new director, and I'm worried that the personnel committee won't do it "right" (meaning, of course, that they won't do it as I would). I imagine that the board will become conservative and ineffective in my absence. I have that slightly confused sense I get when I'm being a mite thought-disordered: I can't quite tell where reality is. I can't possibly have been as central as I tell myself; what did I really contribute?

Leaving the board is an important transition. This organization has filled a variety of needs for me. It's been my political work, my social contribution, my feminist community, my connection to the "real world" that balances the somewhat rarefied atmosphere of a therapy practice. Thinking about what to put in its place has made me realize how well suited my passions and talents are for this particular kind of work. Since leaving, I've had to avoid the impulse to sign up for every possibility that presents itself. The fact that I have to pay attention to that is instructive; I'm not sure I would have guessed how important it is to me to be making some kind of change-the-world contribution. Jeez, you'd think doing therapy full-time would take care of that sort of thing! But it's not the same.

So what comes next? I want to do something that works toward cultural changes which have to do with women. The work needs to be feminist in its process, not just its intent, which probably means some kind of grassroots effort. What I have to offer are my organizational skills, my political analysis, good judgment, and articulateness. Pretty amorphous, I must admit. And my criteria sound awfully specific. But it does feel like if I keep my eyes on what I want, and am thoughtful about it, the right opportunity will come along. After all, there's a lot of work to be done in the world.

JANUARY 1994

A follow-up note, so as not to leave the reader dangling: It's funny, the way life has of taking unexpected turns. It's like that mysterious warning to be careful what you wish for, because you may get it. Meaning, of course, that it may come in a form that you had never anticipated, as well as that it may not mean what you had expected from the safe distance of wishing. I'm reminded of a client who returned to see me after a long hiatus. She'd had years of difficulty in relationships with hurtful men and was comfortably single when she'd last left therapy. She'd kept praying, though, she told me, asking God to "send me someone to love." Was she ever surprised, she announced, when God sent her a woman! "I guess I didn't specify gender!" she laughed.

I'd assumed, when I wrote this, that I would find something very similar to my prior community work. I see that I specified parameters suggesting that. What I got was the editorship of a feminist professional journal. Surprise! From the vantage point of July 1989, I *never* would have imagined that; I'm still a bit astonished to find myself here. I'd written one article for publication by that point. That article came about when a colleague asked me to write about how I approach therapy, and my immediate response was, "I can't possibly put that into words." She said, "Okay, just write something about why it can't be put into words." (And to think this woman does not consider herself a clinician!) So I began to write, and I found in the process that I had, well, just a *bit* more to say about therapy than why it's not easily put into words. Three or four years later I had started these essays. A couple of years after that I was asked to co-edit a collection of writing by previously unpublished authors for a special issue of the same journal. And now I have taken on co-editing the journal, working with the same colleague who had slyly encouraged me into writing my first piece.

Editing a feminist professional journal has much of what I was looking for, after all. It is profoundly political work, although that may not be immediately evident to the reader. An editor has power, and I have the opportunity to use that power to influence what comes into print, encouraging writing by members of marginalized groups, pulling together collections on topics that are seen too infrequently in print. Editing is also an unreasonable amount of work for someone already with a full-time job, and I have agreed to only three years (more like five years, by the time you get started and wind down). Like raising a child or doing therapy, editing is a delight as well as a burden. I too shall be careful what I wish for in the future!

Courage

Well, I believe I'm actually being stood up. The woman who's not here just changed her appointment time (at her request), and that confusion may be part of the problem. She's also quite frightened and extremely ambivalent about therapy, which is more likely the heart of the matter. She can barely stand to bring her pain and need into the room. Each session is similar. We circle each other. "What is it?" I ask. She is torn between wanting the connection and wanting to dance away, keep it light.

Then, as she moves toward the hurt, her struggle begins in earnest. Her whole being conveys the battle: it takes everything in her not to cry. She tries to speak and almost hyperventilates in her effort to overcome her reluctance. No, reluctance is too weak a word. What this looks like is a fight to the death: the absolute necessity of being "strong" and independent is battling her yearning for contact and comfort, and all of it is overlaid with her terror at what she thinks that need means. She is in agony at my responsiveness to her, a responsiveness she has been starving for her whole life. She is horrified at how much I matter to her. I am horrified at what it costs her to let me matter to her and at what that implies about how she's been injured. She calls herself a coward; I am in awe of her courage.

A colleague commented once about the lengths I go to in helping people feel safe in therapy. There's truth in that. For some people it's relatively easy, and my integrity provides safety enough. But for others, "safety enough" is barely imaginable as a concept. And I do feel acutely aware of that, of what it takes for clients to open themselves to me, of what a gift that is. It's not surprising; so much of my own struggle has been in that area. Can I let someone see what hurts me? Scarier still, could I let someone take care of me emotionally? Competence was highly valued in my family; whining was not encouraged. Maybe I keep doing therapy in an effort to learn that it's a good thing for someone to show her or his pain and get cared for. I believe that to be true for everyone else. I wonder how many clients it will take before I'm convinced that it applies to me?

Failure

I got one of those humbling reminders the other day, keeping me mindful of how little I know about the effect I'm having. This was a client I've seen for about six months, someone who's been difficult from the word go. She entered almost immediately into a transference relationship with me, imagining me as her controlling and withholding mother. Now, usually I feel pretty loose in therapy, unaffected by people's ideas about who I am and how I'll fail them or hurt them. But this one got to me. Everything I did was wrong—that is, when she would shut up long enough to let me do anything! I tried one approach after another, assuming that it was simply a matter of finding the right way in, the way that was safe enough for her, that didn't trigger her pain. As I sat with her hour after hour, having my efforts at empathy slapped down, my suggestions for movement dismissed and distorted, my reaching out responded to with hostility and denial, I began to get angry. I didn't like her; I felt helpless and ineffective. In my discouragement, I began to withdraw.

Then I got it: oh, now I *am* her mother indeed—ungiving, unloving, in some kind of battle for control. I struggled to get past it. Enlightening as the insight was, it didn't change much of how I felt. Now I worked each hour not to find a way to "help" her but to find a way to feel warmly toward her, to feel friendly and giving when my impulse was hostile withholding. Talking to her about how I saw it helped a little—helped me a little, that is. It made no difference to her, entrenched as she was in her inability to know what hurt her. I managed a trickle of warmth; pathetic, but something. I felt as though I was failing miserably.

Then she told me that she wanted to stop coming. *Of course,* I thought, *given what a crummy job I'm doing with her.* It certainly seemed like the best decision to me: she wasn't getting good therapy and, besides, I had to admit I'd be at least somewhat glad to see her go. I asked what she wanted for closure. As people often do, she wanted to review what she'd come for and what she'd accomplished. She talked about her self-image, about how much better she was feeling about herself. Huh? Well, now that I thought of it, she *had* seemed more positive lately, had even made an important change in her life that was directly related to meeting her needs. She had said she wanted to stop coming for reasons of time and money pressures, very much in character for someone who insisted on externalizing much of her pain, seeing the reasons for her distress as "out there" and beyond her control. But then she asked me how I saw her. Among my remarks, I mentioned that she was hurt from not getting enough nurturing. She commented that she knew she tended to run away from real nurturing. So there it was. She was leaving therapy because—surprise!—I evidently had succeeded, at least enough, in nurturing her. Knowing she could never accept a direct response, I responded in kind, that is, in metaphor, giving her permission to take it slowly, to back off, to learn to tolerate love step by step.

Well, whaddaya know. My failure was only a failure relative to my standards, relative to my own expectation for myself of a fully loving response. Compared to this woman's expectation of extreme and unremitting withholding, my pittance was quite a lot. Of course, what particularly made it a lot had to do with how successful she had been in turning me into her mother in the first place. In fact, I had started the work with her in the state of fairly full responsiveness that I usually start with, but that didn't count, didn't touch her. Only when she had stopped me from responding, making our relationship into a repeat of the hopeless one that she'd had with her mother, did the response I managed (limited though it was) mean something. It meant that all was not lost, that her mother could learn to love her, that she was worthy of being cared for.

Now, I have no illusions about this particular woman; her journey has barely begun. She has a long road ahead of her and a difficult one, both for herself and for any person who chooses to accompany her. But now I realize that I have, in fact, helped her make a start. She did that difficult initial push with me, and the door opened just a crack. Perhaps from there she can begin to see a way out. For myself, I am reminded once again that a client's accomplishments are measured by his or her own yardstick, not by mine.

Feeding the Soul

One of those luminous late summer days today, the planet moving toward fall. There's something stirring about the transitional seasons, an excitement and aliveness that I don't experience with winter or summer, the seasons of being rather than changing. Sometimes I think I don't take enough advantage of the outdoors here. I move between my office and my home, enclosed spaces, while outside the air is sweetly delicious, the clouds and the hilltops make love, the forest winks at me and calls my name. I go backpacking the week after next, and my responsiveness is heightened in anticipation. In the meantime, the drive to work will have to do.

I don't realize how hungry I get spiritually until I'm on the brink of my annual stint in the woods, which is my primary way of meeting that hunger. Then I get this fierce longing, partly for the forest itself but mostly for the soul nourishment that always seems to come with my time there. Kind of a difficult and time-consuming way to get a spiritual experience, I think, but the only thing I've found so far that works. I don't think I've done very well in the spiritual department, especially given how important that is to me. I do tend to have a consistent awareness of that dimension in my everyday life, but when it comes to evoking it specifically, I'm really at a loss. It's similar to having this palpable companion in my life that dissolves as soon as I try to call it to me. But maybe the point, of course, is that you can't call the spirit to you like some trained dog. As with the light of late August, you instead must live inside it.

Coming Home

I just returned from my annual backpacking trip. Such a condensed experience. This year, as always, it was difficult—painful and even frightening—in some ways, intensely lovely in others. I sat by a lake and listened to loons calling; I watched a fawn watch me in the wet woods early one morning; I sang with my hiking companion for hours as the night deepened.

And, as always, I emerge from the woods quieted. The texture of that quiet is different each time, but it's always there—not just a still point inside but a stillness that fills me and goes past my edges and is held in common. For someone such as myself, whose usual inner state is just a little too active, this is a profoundly altered state of consciousness.

Nature is inconvenient, you know. Its temperature is often uncomfortable, its weather disruptive and occasionally dangerous. It is dirty. And tending to the body's demands can be so tedious. "This hurts; do something," it whines. "Eat this but not that. I'm thirsty. Pee soon. Tired; go to sleep." Civilized life is so much more comfortable, so much easier. How wonderful to be able to protect the body from nature's vagaries and from its own sharp needs. How luxurious then to have one's attention free for other things—for the complexities of civilized life, for example. To live in the woods for a time with only what can be carried on my back is intentionally to strip away the comfort and control that protect me (and wall me off) from nature. Although I enjoy being outside at other times, those are essentially quite controlled experiences: to walk outside when the weather's nice is to keep nature as an adjunct to my own experience, with myself still at the center. But to live outside day after day is to experience nature as central. My small barriers of sleeping bag or dry socks are so minor when compared to my usual protection of a house with a hot shower.

When I hike in the rain, my first response is to run for cover. "Eeek! I'm wet! I'm wet!" yells the body. But there is no cover. I'm in the real world, remember, not my contrived world. Eventually I accept, my body accepts, that if it rains I'll get wet. It might even feel good. With the consistent force of pressure that nature acquires under these circumstances, I have no choice but to give in. My sense of myself as ending at my skin fades, my boundaries diffuse. My illusion of centrality and control dwindle down to something small and silly. I talk less; I laugh more and louder. I live in and for my body. Where else? Why else?

Christmas As a Defense Mechanism

DECEMBER 17, 1989

Into the dark of the year; nightfall at 4:30. And that's if it's clear. On cloudy days the lamp in my office is on by 3:00, 3:30. Snow has taken its place as a primary element in our lives. It drapes itself in soft folds over the landscape, against my windows. It's the medium, like air, through which we move. Snow as female: powerful, lovely, compelling, and dangerous if disregarded.

I'm feeling a bit alienated about Christmas. Oh, I like the stuff of it—the lights, even the presents, singing, and feasting. And I can't help this gleeful astonishment that we get to bring a *tree* into the house and hang gewgaws on it. This is *socially sanctioned* behavior. Who would have imagined? But it feels as though we're doing the right things for the wrong reasons, that we're missing the point.

Outside I can almost hear the scary rumble of the earth moving toward the solstice. The walls of my home seem flimsy protection from the vast night and deepening cold. Christmas as psychic defense: manic merrymaking to avoid coming to terms with the season's lessons of death and loss. Reaction formation. Alternatively, Christmas as an act of courage. Hope in June is cheap.

Many of my clients (and other people too, of course) are distressed at this time of year, but again for the wrong reasons. They talk about holiday stress and family expectations. True enough, but not the half of it. The earth itself is a metaphor, speaking to us in its language of darkness and retreat. If we gave the truth a chance to emerge, we'd be profoundly disturbed. Or maybe we are; but who could tell with all those cookies that need to be baked, all those parties to attend? Perhaps we'd be better off if we just let ourselves get good and despairing, if we gave up, if we acknowledged our fears and mourned our losses. Then at least we'd have the possibility of some kind of authentic change, like the earth's delicate shifting of balance, a minute at a time, slowly and inevitably toward the light.

ଓ *1990* ଔ

Faking It

I've been sick the past few days, and decided to work most of the time in spite of how I feel. The whole calculation about whether to stay home is certainly different from what I would do in a "regular" job. If I stay home, after all, (1) I won't get paid; (2) my absence affects people emotionally; and (3) *I'm* the one who has to call people and listen to their disappointment, just when I feel least prepared to make any additional effort. Almost easier just to drag myself into the office. After all, it is a "desk job," isn't it? Besides, work is a great distraction. Maybe I won't notice how awful I feel if I'm paying attention to someone else.

Only, of course, it doesn't quite work that way. Time drags, it's hard to concentrate, my body distracts me from my clients instead of the other way around. I feel like a grounded bird. My instincts are clouded, so I try to compensate by bringing a greater effort of will to the work, willing myself to attend, to think. But intent is no substitute for intuition, and thinking has very little to do with good therapy. The work grinds along without fluidity or inspiration, a mundane effortful sort of concoction that is helpful only in small calculated ways.

My symptoms until today have been of the invisible sort (pain, slight fever, low energy) and therefore not especially evident to others. Now I'm congested and sound like a frog, so I'll be advertising my condition (ribbit!). Most interesting are the client responses on either end of the spectrum: those who feel driven to take care of me and those who are self-absorbed enough not to notice at all.

For me, this is one of those times (the other is before I go on vacation) when I am most keenly aware of the work I do as just that: work. It's a job, I work hard at it, I get paid. I notice a small sour note of something like resentment, or maybe it's impatience. My shift's not up yet; I'm putting in my time. I feel slightly guilty. People deserve something more wholehearted than this. Still, most of the time they get it. And if sometimes I can pull rabbits out of hats, then there will be those times when the best I can come up with is ribbits. (Ha. Being sick has affected my sense of humor. A brain virus, no doubt.) It will have to do.

The Witness Protection Program

FEBRUARY 15, 1990

One of the funny (from a considerable distance, that is) and frustrating things about small-town practice is the practical limit to confidentiality. At the board meeting of the local shelter for battered women, the program director outlines a situation involving the state attorney's response to a rape victim. No name or identifying information is mentioned, of course, but it seems that half the people present know exactly the situation we're discussing. Unlike therapy, the prosecution of a rape is a public event. A lawyer on the board comments on her involvement with the woman. Someone has discussed the problem with the clerk in the state attorney's office and can offer the inside perspective. A neighbor to the woman puts in her two cents. It's impossible to discuss policy without sounding like neighbors at a church supper, gossiping over the latest news. It was amazing to me as a therapist, since we small-town clinicians learn to be almost paranoid about confidentiality. But this was not therapists, and it showed something about just how interlocked our lives are in a rural area.

My office mate's clients say hello to me on the street and in the waiting room, although I try assiduously to avoid their eyes. I have become quite adept at walking into the waiting room and then maneuvering my body so that I can greet the person waiting for me without looking at the one who isn't. If that seems extreme, consider that my colleague's clients are my neighbors, my clients' current or ex-lovers, the shopkeepers who know my name and purchasing habits, sometimes even my own friends, acquaintances, or colleagues. Sometimes the dissimulation becomes impossible and I give up all hope of pretense with one person or another, plunking myself down in a waiting-room chair to chat until it's time for his or her therapy session.

Trying to consult with my office partner in this context is like some kind of psychic ballet. Mostly we're fairly graceful about it, stepping easily around certain kinds of information, saying just enough. Usually if the therapy is feeling off with a particular person, the important data are about the therapist anyway. When, in spite of myself, I put things together enough to identify someone, I'm quite capable of filing that knowledge somewhere marked "I don't know this," so that it's not a problem. Denial is a wonderfully effective tool.

Recently, I needed to talk about a situation that involved someone that I know who is too connected to this colleague to risk any possibility of identification. Now what? One other therapist in town might do as a consultant if I gave her careful instruction about how to be helpful. She's rarely available and our relationship is such that the whole business would be complicated. I don't think there's anyone else in town I could approach who would have a clue about where to begin. I know I can get what I need from this colleague, and she's right down the hall. . . .

So, I try to talk about what the problem is without saying what the problem is. Sounds fine, we agree, I'll just talk about it without any content. Long silence. "Well," I say, "it's that . . ." *Can't say that,* I announce to myself in my head. "I've noticed how she . . ." *Oops, cancel, cancel,* says the inner censor. More silence. Hmmm. Separating my responses from the person involved is not as simple as it sounded. I finally manage to say a few vague things about how I feel. My consultant's initial efforts to respond are way off base, founded on assumptions that don't apply in this case, for reasons I'm not free to reveal. We eventually figure out how to fumble our way through this, with my making statements that are more symbolic of the issues than expressive of them, and my consultant saying enough back to indicate permissive accompaniment. Even when I get to a point of some resolution, I can't say what my internal discovery is for fear of implying something about the person whose identity I'm working so hard to protect.

Sometimes I wonder about this business of being a therapist in this setting. The profession itself requires a great deal of circumspection in any case, but practice in a rural setting multiplies that geometrically.

To be a rural therapist means the chronic self-awareness that comes with never feeling anonymous. It means that you can never really be separate from your work. It enforces habitual secrecy.

It's common wisdom that people choose professions that suit their personalities; what's less often discussed are the ways that our work, in turn, shapes who we become. Some of how therapy shapes me seems benign or even positive. I'm sure I've become more intuitive, more self-aware. I've seen enough of human nature to have learned a deep acceptance of our weaknesses and a humble appreciation of our tenacity. But other lessons from work seem more worrisome, such as the edict to be careful what you say, be careful what you do. Being a therapist teaches circumspection, enforces more dignity than is perhaps good for anyone. Perhaps in my retirement I'll become a professional fool and restore the balance.

Visibility

Four clients or former clients were at Town Meeting last week. A couple of them avoided me, one sought me out to tell me how her life is going, one was just normal. And then there were the people who aren't clients but whose relationship to me has a little extra charge, almost like transference, because of the work I do. An example is the sister of a client who went through an extended crisis period. The sister knows my role in helping the client get through the crisis, and she is a little in awe of that.

Everyone gives away information about themselves when they speak at Town Meeting: where they stand on an issue, how they handle themselves. But when I get up to speak, it's often with a particular edge of self-awareness. I'm not just a neighbor and citizen. I know that some people in the room are filtering what I say through their hopes and needs and old family relationships. I imagine that it's a small taste of the experience of celebrities or other public figures. At first it's seductive, to feel so important. But then it simply feels like a burden, this artificial importance that has so little to do with me. It's like being surrounded by a thick fog of other people's expectations; the real me is invisible in it. It's usually not all that big a deal, just one element in my awareness. But once in a while, when I feel it more heavily, I long for anonymity, to be judged only by who I am. It's an odd sense of constraint, since by nature I tend to act with forethought anyway. But with the pressure to consider the effects of my behavior, I perversely want to be careless, to be an asshole and have it mean nothing more than a minor irritation to those listening.

At the gym a few days ago, I ran into a former client whom I occasionally see there. I wonder how effective I was with her, thinking that I wasn't all that helpful and imagining that she feels the same. We smiled at each other, both of us wanting to make it clear how adult and fine we are. Later, in the locker room, I saw another former client. Our work together was okay, but not great. I don't think she really got what she needed from me. We exchanged pleasantries in a mildly constrained way before I stripped down to head for the shower. Maybe it's some kind of karmic reparations to have to get naked in front of the people I failed. Yup, here I am in my somewhat flawed body, a match for the somewhat flawed therapy I did with you.

Although sharing a locker room with clients seems as though it would be the height of awkwardness, usually it's not too bad. I'm habituated to the setting, and often less self-conscious than the other person. Usually we get through it with some friendly chatter. Occasionally, the incongruity is even funny. One time an acquaintance took the opportunity to ask about starting therapy with me. I didn't have a stitch on. Did she think I had my appointment book tucked under one breast, perhaps? Luckily, I didn't giggle at all, but responded as if it were a perfectly reasonable question. So much for the adage that clothes make the (wo)man!

Weightlessness

MAY 10, 1990

I got a call this weekend from a woman who was a client, oh, maybe four or five years ago. Maybe it's longer. She's come in occasionally for a "tune-up" in the intervening years, although I don't think I've talked to her in more than a year now.

Anyway, what struck me about talking with her again was how incredibly valuable our connection is. She was pretty stuck and depressed when she called. It didn't take us all that long to shift it. But we had a lot to draw on. We have a history together. She trusts me and knows how to get to where the trouble is. I know her language, her worldview, what metaphors will touch her. I don't have to spend time learning who she is or what works. She doesn't have to spend time learning what works or getting safety. Like familiar dance partners, we move together comfortably and with grace. How easy therapy is, how satisfying, when you don't have to struggle with all that testing of the waters!

It feels the way I imagine it would be to conduct an orchestra (once you were good at it). Its complexity requires all of you: body, feelings, spirit, and mind. Its delicacy demands absolute proficiency, complete attention. Yet the experience is one of effortlessness. I once read that a famous conductor was asked what he thought about when he was conducting. His reply was that he thought about dinner. I don't think about dinner, but what's closest to the truth is that I don't think at all. What a pleasure.

Identity

This has been one of my days "off," which is really just unstructured work instead of scheduled work. I've worked on several professional projects, had one work-related meeting, saw a client (since I was in town for the meeting anyway and couldn't seem to find any other time to see her), and did other odds and ends. The fact that it's my day off means that I get to do most of this at home, where I can also do a couple of loads of laundry at the same time. I've started keeping track of the non–office work I do, curious how much it adds up to. Today it adds up to plenty.

I had a funny little contrast yesterday. One of my clients was talking about a couple's therapist she had gone to. She was struck by the therapist's style, which was forthright to the point of blunt. My client wasn't sure she liked that and noted that it was quite different from her experience with me, since I was so gentle and careful with her. The following hour, I was making arrangements with the next client to talk with her briefly on the phone. She said that she was reluctant to call me at home, and I reassured her that she wouldn't disturb me because if she called at a bad time I would just tell her so and we would find another time to talk. She gave a relieved smile and said, "That's what I like about you, you're so direct and up front."

Pretty amusing, huh? Are they talking about the same person? The thing is, both are right. The first woman is someone who's very traumatized and can barely tolerate therapy, even with all the gentleness and caution I can muster. The second woman is a down-to-earth person who speaks her mind; with her, I do too, and thus we understand each other. It's just a reminder of the immense variability of therapy, even with the same therapist. One really has to be a chameleon, oneself always, but changing with the emotional tone, needs, and personal style of the other individual. Thirty clients, thirty different therapies, thirty different therapists.

The other thing I have been thinking about is a bit harder to describe. I was talking with a client about how real self-love is not selfish or egocentric because it is not about one's accomplishments or "doings." Selfishness is about possession—in this case, possession of successes or achievements, glory, vanity. Self-love is about one's "being." I remember hearing or reading about an exercise in which the participants wrote on pieces of paper their various definitions of themselves, for example, I am a woman, I am a white person, I am a mother, I am a nurse. Each person arranged the definitions in a pile from those they were least attached to, to those that were more central to their identity. Then, starting with the least central definition, these individuals would try to imagine giving it up as a way they defined themselves. When they felt they could do that, could imagine and accept themselves without that definition, they would throw that piece of paper on the floor in front of them. Then they would do the same with the next most important one, and so on until they had "thrown away" all of their usual ways of defining themselves. Who were they then? What were they left with? I have not done the exercise, but I can imagine how scary it would be. And how liberating. One would be left with one's essence, the light that is the particular aspect of life, of divinity, that is the individual at this moment. *That* is what one loves when one loves oneself. And that, like any other form of worship (I mean that word in the sense of recognition of the sacred), is a selfless act.

It occurs to me that by that definition, doing good therapy is a form of worship. (I need a different word, *Worship* has too many associations that make me annoyed.) Good therapy involves a love of the essence of the other, completely outside of the person's achievements and failings. That's the heart of what's so satisfying to me about therapy. And it's kind of reassuring to have articulated that: As I've (partially!) outgrown some of my more "neurotic" reasons for liking to do therapy, I've wondered with some anxiety what might be left to motivate me to do the work. I've recognized that I find satisfaction in just doing skillful work, and some satisfaction in other ways (the closeness, the sense of contribution). But none of that seemed quite enough. This does.

The main time I have that experience of my own essence, of course, is when I'm backpacking. It's the exhaustion, probably, but also that in the woods I am only the walker—not the psychologist, not my various other self-descriptions. I am reminded of something from Eva Hoffman's *Lost in Translation*. She describes the pain of being caught between two languages and of being freed from that struggle as she falls asleep: "How strange, I think, how strange what I've become, and then words cease and, in my drowsiness, I've become an animal thing I've always known, only myself." Exactly.

Heal Thyself

I had a dream recently, the closest thing to a nightmare I've had in years. Good shrink that I am (A primary rule of shrinkdom: Stay on top of your own stuff. Not that any of us ever get higher than a B– in this department), I made some time to sort through what the dream was telling me. Yuck, bad news. There it was, the worst of how I feel stuck. My response was predictable: I felt awful. And naturally, feeling awful, I got more stuck. *Coward,* I told myself. Maybe I have to feel even worse before I'll make the changes I should. Not a happy prospect.

This afternoon I was vaguely thinking about work. I remembered a client I saw yesterday, a woman who's incredibly hard on herself. She's one of those people who responded to family chaos by getting too competent too young, and now she's got no margin for error in her life. Perfect is barely good enough. As you can imagine, this is an effective but fairly exhausting solution. Out of the blue, I suggested that she make a refrigerator chart, the kind that children have for doing their chores. Since this woman has small children of her own, she could relate to this. "Stickers!" I said with enthusiasm. "You can give yourself a sticker every time you make a mistake!" She caught on to the spirit of the occasion. "Yes, and a treat when I get a certain number of stickers!" We were off and running, conspiring together. Her "problem" had become a source of both entertainment and reward.

Then I think about another client, a woman who has come a long way and was now confronting that kind of bottom-line fear that people often have about changing who they are in a profound way. Existential terror, that's what it looks like to me: How can I live, who will I be if I am no longer the person I have always been? A couple of months ago, she recounted a dream, actually two linked dreams, that frightened her badly. Both featured natural disasters, scary indeed. Yet oddly enough, the outcome of these disasters was not destruction, but rather lovely images of comfort and tranquility. I saw the dreams as showing her the truth about her own dilemma: what looks like disaster and certain death is, in reality, the way toward the best of what she hopes for.

With these thoughts idly in my mind, I suddenly got a clear sense of how unhelpful I had been to myself about my own situation. In life, as in therapy, it's easy to focus on what's the matter. I can get stuck in this notion that whatever's wrong is somehow more true than whatever's right. And the more I feel that way, the less able I am to do anything to change it. Now it seems so obvious. I wasn't thinking of these two clients just at random, I was trying to get a message to myself. Hey, do you suppose you could interpret that dream in another way, a way with humor, with possibility? What about changing how you look at this big heavy "problem"—that's what you do with other people. Are you listening? Luckily, I was. As if to emphasize the point, as I was scribbling some notes to myself about all of this (in hopes of remembering for next time, just in case I'm so on top of things as to remember to look at them), I was interrupted by an impossible racket outside. I tore down the stairs, and there they were, a whole flock of geese heading south, flying low, the afternoon sun like honey on their wings.

Doing It for Free

My brief talk with a friend about values yesterday brings to mind a client who definitely is not living by the rules. He moves from job to job, delivering papers, helping with logging, doing occasional tutoring (he's good with math), and lives in a tiny trailer without plumbing. Last year he made $3,100, which he considers an immense amount of money. Most of his energy goes into just keeping his life going. His way of living means that he is subject to all kinds of hassles that more settled people avoid. Naturally, this inclines me to make various shrinky hypotheses: Is he sabotaging himself? Does he keep his life chaotic for a reason? Does he want to be rescued? I really don't think so. His life mostly works for him. He has, in fact, kept himself alive and well for some time now, and this is someone who is fifty-six years old. He's made a lot of changes in therapy, but becoming what he disparagingly calls "bouggie" (bourgeois) was not one of his goals, and has not been one of his changes. And who am I to say it should be?

He rarely pays me. Officially, I'm keeping a tab, but I don't expect to see it. We've been around a number of times on the matter of payment, and I've come to the conclusion that he simply doesn't think that way. (This is congruent with lots of other ways in which his thought patterns are unusual.) I don't know—maybe it's secretly manipulative and a boundary issue, although he's not problematic about boundaries in other ways and it doesn't feel manipulative. It does drive me nuts periodically. Occasionally he pays me a bit; mostly he doesn't. The whole business makes me wonder which of us is off about values: the client who can't quite comprehend paying my bill or the therapist who thinks that someone with an annual income of $3,100 should pay even $20 an hour to talk to her?

I know the official reasoning: Clients should pay for therapy as a symbolic investment in themselves and in the work they're doing. The fee creates a clear line between therapist and client, making it obvious that this is not a friendship. But people with Medicaid or with good insurance sometimes pay nothing. They don't seem any less committed to their therapy or particularly confused about the nature of the therapy relationship. This man does not have the luxury of insurance or virtually any disposable income, yet he pays me when he can. Is that less responsible?

Another client was talking with me recently about the phenomenon of finding that she was actually making good money. How surprising and wonderful, yet she also has that slight sense of it being vaguely shameful and a feeling of wanting to keep it a secret. How will this affect her relationships with friends who earn much less? What is a person supposed to do with money after he or she has taken care of the necessities? Buy luxuries? How much luxury is "deserved" and when does it become unconscionable? Should the women give it away? Save it? How is she to balance her sense of social obligation with her need for security? And who does a person get to talk to about this? She kept saying what a relief it was just to be able to say her confused feelings without worrying about my being judgmental or envious. Money is just as dirty a secret as sex.

Neighbors

Election day. I can't wait for it to be over so that all those politicians will *shut up!* I'm sick of television and radio ads. In my small town, the best way for anyone running for office to meet the populace is to hang around the garbage truck on dump day. Now, that seems just fine to me. They can hardly be pompous standing by the garbage truck with their signs and brochures. And if I'd like to talk with one of them, I can choose to do so (they're usually terribly grateful), and if I don't care to talk, I just look surly and elbow on by with my bags of trash, like warding off vampires with garlic.

Voting today after work was the quintessence of the small-town experience. The voting booths are wooden, with homemade burlap curtains, a small shelf, and a pencil. The women checking the voter registration list always confuse me with another woman in town whose hair is like mine. My neighbor stops me on the way out to ask, "Did you vote straight Republican?"—a running joke between us, as he knows full well my political leanings, having been at any number of town meetings with me. Another neighbor plays the foil: "Well, I don't even know any straight Republicans," giving the first man the opportunity to say, grinning, arm around his wife, "*I'm* a straight Republican!"

The reference to sexual orientation makes me remember that two of the elected town officials are lesbians. Interesting for a conservative small town. Everyone knows these women are lesbians, but no one ever says anything about it. They mind their own business. My guess is that many people in town who might be officially homophobic simply don't think about these women "that way." They are neighbors, and the rest can be overlooked. Not exactly enlightened, but a live-

and-let-live attitude that makes some sense of cohesion possible in a rural area where neighbors have to depend on one another. There are animosities, of course. But it is hard to write anyone off completely when that person may be the one who helps to pull your car out of a snowbank during the next storm. If only countries operated the same way!

Zen Landscape

I drove up the interstate last weekend, after this year's first real snow: instant winter. In spite of all the aggravation that winter represents—cold, driving hassles, six months of feeling housebound, and dark, dark—there's still something so compelling, a rightness that strikes me as the season starts. It's visual: the colors muted; a no-frills palette of white and soft pastels, blue shadows on the snow, gray and dark green. The eye sweeps across the horizon undistracted by summer's jumble of leaves, vivid color, layers of texture sprouting everywhere, muchness. Winter's minimalism forces me to attend to subtlety, to nuance. To quiet.

Like the desert, I thought as I was driving. That's what's so appealing to me about the desert: the hidden aliveness, a rich emptiness. Zen landscape. What comes to mind is how I heard one woman describe the tundra: the land spread out "like an altar." On the car's tape player I heard Libana sing a round that spoke precisely to this feeling: "winter calls a clear horizon . . . like the sky calls to the desert"— whew, yes. I know that by February at least, or January, or maybe even sooner, if I read this again I'll want to give myself the raspberry. I'll be crazed with cabin fever and this will all sound like horsepucky. But now even the increasing darkness feels right, feels sacred.

What's It Worth?

DECEMBER 3, 1990

I've decided to raise my fees, always a tough one. I called a colleague this morning as I was agonizing about it, checking to see what she charges. Her fee is currently the same as mine, and she was thinking about raising hers, too. She was having the same trouble I was: Fees for psychotherapy are already ridiculously high, how could one possibly justify making them even higher? Yet the reality for both of us is that with the slowed economy we find ourselves taking a greater number of people at significantly reduced fees. She mentioned that she has more clients on Medicaid, which pays less than half the going rate. I know that the insurance companies are disgusted with getting left holding the bag, but the truth is that everyone depends on higher insurance reimbursements to cover for people who have no insurance or inadequate insurance. It may not be fair in business terms, but it's the only solution that's fair in human terms. My fees may be obscenely high when viewed on a real-life comparison basis, but turning away people who can only afford a limited payment or not continuing with clients whose financial fortunes change would be unconscionable.

What's particularly interesting about my colleague is that I happen to know her partner, also a therapist, already charges a fair chunk more than she does. Her partner is a man. I would love to do a survey and find out whether there is a difference between men and women in the amount they charge and the number of people they see at reduced fees, but I suspect the results would only give me one more thing to rant and rave about.

So, although the decision feels right to me from a kind of Robin Hood perspective, I feel slightly guilty with each client that I tell. Partly it's the nature of the work. It's like asking someone to pay you for loving them. But mostly it's my projection of how this must seem to them. If it were me, I would do math in my mind. Let's see, her fee is thus-and-so and she probably has this many clients, so she must be making an immense amount of money. Those calculations don't figure in business expenses, or all those people who aren't paying full fee, or that no therapist in his or her right mind sees anything approaching forty clients a week. But there it is. How can you charge people that much for *talking* to them, for chrissakes? Especially when you expect them to pay it every week? It's exorbitant. *I* couldn't afford to pay my fee, and I make a good living!

If you work for an agency, your salary is what it is, what someone else thinks the work is worth. You can ask for a raise, but it's still between you and the agency. The client, and what the client pays, is kept separate. Imagine asking thirty people for a raise, a raise that must be at least partly paid out of their pockets. You know them well enough to have some idea what financial and personal strain this will add to their lives, what this might mean to them about their wishes to be loved for themselves (i.e., not for pay!), and you have some idea of what's involved. Oh, it's buffered. People know the reality of paying for therapy. With insurance, the actual change in fee that most clients pay is minimal. I haven't changed my fees in years and many of them know it. But still those other currents are there.

It's an odd thing in a way, setting your own salary knowing that the money must come from the people you serve. It adds an element of personal responsibility that people in other kinds of work don't have to face. What is therapy worth? When I'm doing a particularly magnificent job, a melding of heart and intuition and intelligence, it's hard to think of work that requires a higher level of skill. Then it seems that it's worth any amount of pay. When I'm tired and just coasting through, doing okay but nothing special, my fee is a rip off. Most of the time it's somewhere in the middle, work of reasonably high quality but not earth-shattering, relying on experience as much as anything. It makes me think of the story about the plumber who fixed something with just a few taps from a hammer. When asked to itemize the apparently unreasonable bill of $50 for a few minutes' work, the plumber replies, "Well, that's fifty cents for the tapping and forty-nine fifty for knowing where to tap." I guess that about covers it.

ది *1991* ౪

Back to Kindergarten

JANUARY 16, 1991

Naturally, what's on my mind about work is the workshop on hypnosis that I just returned from. It was three intensive days that I soaked up thirstily, and my psyche has been working overtime to integrate it all. Last night was the first night I've slept reasonably well in four or five days now. I've been dreaming nonstop about hypnosis and talking about it obsessively to friends. I've been thinking with every client, *Hmmm, would hypnosis be helpful to this person? In what way?* And here I am writing about it too. My, what a hell of a lot of work, this integration stuff! I can feel the temptation to forget it, to let the experience become one more interesting workshop, and the tools become rusty objects that I pull out of my bag of tricks once in a while with hesitation. Tempting to just let it go because I can tell that to assimilate the knowledge in a way that is truly useful in my work, I still have a lot more to do. I have to get the techniques practiced and habitual enough that I don't have to think about them at all. I need to get experience with a broad range of responses to hypnosis so that the individual differences in people's experiences are familiar to me. And I need to get enough experience with making use of the altered state so that its possibilities, structure, and language become second nature. Only then will I be able to use it with ease and skill. Achieving all of that is a *lot* of work! Furthermore, it feels as though I have to do it now, and fairly intensively, while the material is fresh in my mind. I don't think I'll learn it well if I just practice a little now and then.

It makes me aware of how much I have to know as a therapist, and know so well that I can forget about knowing it. I can't attend to subtleties of process if I'm having to think consciously about use of language or technique or struggle to place a person's responses in some kind of larger context. It feels strange, after all this time, to experience this degree of not-knowing again. It's odd to be intentional and aware in some cognitive way of what I'm doing, to monitor myself so that I do this or that right, so that I avoid this or that mistake. In fact, it feels worse than the first time around (as a new therapist, I mean), at least in some ways. When I was beginning as a therapist I didn't really know what my goals felt like, so I had no way of knowing how much more skilled and knowledgeable I would have to become to get there. Now I do know all that, so I have no comfy illusions or ignorance to buffer my sense of what it takes to become really good at something this complex. (Not that the "how to" of hypnosis is all that complex. But knowing the uses and manifestations of the state well enough to use it with confidence and precision and fluidity, well, that's another matter.) The good news is that I have a pretty clear idea of how to develop that skill. The bad news is I know all too well that I will be awkward and inadequate and make mistakes—probably nothing ir-revocable, but mistakes nonetheless—with real live human beings along the way. I can minimize that probability, but I can't eliminate it.

That's tough about doing this work, especially for me, with my hy-peractive sense of responsibility. Oh, I make mistakes anyway, out of countertransference or sloppiness or even occasionally ignorance. But mostly I feel skilled enough, the "good-enough mother." I don't relish the prospect of feeling like the "just scraping by and making it up as I go along" mother!

The Bright Line

I'm working with a woman who was seriously hurt and neglected as a child. . . . I realize even as I write this how futile it feels to try to describe the extent of her hurt. Where to begin? It's similar to the feeling of the person who approaches therapy for the first time. How do I start? I could chronicle the specific and individual horrors I know her to have been subjected to—the ones I know about, that is. They are only a small portion of the ones she remembers, which in turn are only a fragment of her actual history. Maybe a more immediate indicator of the way she was damaged is to talk about how much she doesn't remember.

I recall, as a young adolescent, that when something hurtful happened at home I would sometimes say to myself, *I don't want to remember this.* And I would push it out of my mind, out of my feelings, refusing to give it attention until it curled up and slipped silently to some back corner of my experience. I used to think that such things were gone; now I know better. I know that I may not keep a memory, but I keep the experience, embedded in the way I understand reality, influencing how I approach and back off, printed on my body. What is forgotten is often far more powerful than what is remembered.

Anyway, this client came to me "missing" huge gaps of her history. Imagine what must have happened to make it necessary for her to erase her own background. And imagine what that must cost her, not to know what she's done, not to know what was done to her.

I've been meeting with her for some time now. I know that where she's been neglected, I've been reliable and responsive; where she's felt worthless, I've taken her seriously; where she's come to expect pain and betrayal, I've been consistently caring. And that is much of the task of therapy for someone damaged as brutally and early as she: to experience a relationship that provides a different template of the possibilities for human connection. Like a small child, she drinks it up. Also like a small child, she has fallen in love with her mother—me.

Transference is a complicated thing. It is easy for a child and mother to manage the child's possessive love, his or her wish to marry mommy. It's not so easy when the "child" is a grown person. My client argues persuasively that she knows enough about me to love me. Indeed, she knows a lot about my character. She knows what makes me laugh, what moves me, my political views, and my values. Yet while I have shared deeply of who I am in some ways, I have offered little in others. She doesn't know much about my history or my personal life or how I spend my time. She knows little of my own joys and hurts, of what feels risky to me, how I receive love, or how I open to another in a mutual relationship. That's the key. Our relationship has is some important ways not been mutual. What's difficult is that in other ways it's been very mutual. A mother exchanges so much with her child. She both gives and receives. Yet our parents' lives are so often mysterious to us; an impossible gulf separates the generations.

To step over this gulf, to agree to true mutuality with this client, would be to destroy the very thing that has begun to heal her. Like a mother taking her child as a lover, it would be a betrayal of the most profound kind. My client imagines that a mutual relationship with me would be similar to what she has now, only more. The truth is that the ways in which the relationship is not mutual are what make it possible for me to be the best caregiver that I am able. Because my needs have so minor a place in our relationship, I can focus fully on hers. I can be consistently loving without the complications of how I might inject my own expectations and disappointments. The truth is that while I love my friends wholeheartedly and well, I love my clients more "purely," if you will. I save my neuroses for my other relation-ships—or, more accurately, neuroses only become a factor when my own confused web of hopes and desires and sorrows are entangled with those of the other person. My clients get a simpler love. Who wouldn't want more of it?

The Cost of Silence

I am back from an acquaintance's funeral and feeling (predictably) melancholy. Every loss reminds me of every other loss, a parade of people I've loved, people I miss. My experience is reasonably normative, I imagine, and the parade isn't too long—yet. I can't imagine how I'll manage the accumulation in twenty years, in thirty. What do people do?

I'm at loose ends without my partner around, too. It's the combination that does it, I suppose. Temporary loss and permanent loss. I create some extra discomfort for myself by being stubbornly unwilling to distract myself with this chore or that. There's nothing around that I want to read. I want something engaging or nothing at all, so I get nothing. I feel closed down and weighted, a stone on top of a trap door.

Part of what hurt so badly in adolescence was feeling so profoundly isolated. To be in pain and not yet to have a voice for it, not to know how to get companionship or even that companionship was missing, not to know where it hurt or why or what to do but mutely endure. To meet pain with dumb animal stolidness, the bit lip, the tears unwept. Only isolation helped—not as relief, but as respite from assault.

Learning to speak the language of pain has been a triumph to me. It is the gift of my profession. To have skills and knowledge, to know the beast and its habits, and to be able to say its name. No isolation is so profound as that of silence.

Perhaps that's what gets a person through loss: the speaking of it. It's certainly the function of funerals. I remember reading of a Native American tribe in which the tradition was for people who had suffered a major loss to shave their heads. How compassionate and sensible it seemed to me to mark their status clearly as bereaved in a way that others would notice immediately without having to say it. Further, anyone could see at a glance just how far you were from the point of loss. Hair grows slowly. It would be years before you looked "normal," years during which your loss would be a visible and inextricable part of you.

The ritual of a funeral is a good thing, but it is far too limited. I hope that those most touched by this death are able to speak their loss passionately and complexly and repeatedly. I hope that their friends ask them about it not just this week, but in three months, and six, and in a year. I would wish that we might all remember, as we look at one another, that each of us carries injuries no less real for being invisible.

Remembering What's Sacred

JUNE 19, 1991

I drove the back roads home today instead of my usual straight shot up the state roadway. Vermont's hills and pastures are impossibly green. Green, this spring's lesson for us *Sesame Street* adults. I've been catching myself staring foolishly at hillsides, amazed at how differently each tree interprets green. Not wise when you're doing fifty miles an hour. Were there always that many shades of the color? I drove more slowly on the gravel roads today, and tried to let myself soak up the heartbreaking loveliness of the landscape. Little birds popped up out of the hayfields as I went past, jack-in-the-box surprises. We hung on through endless winter, and mud season, and the onslaught of black flies to find ourselves—muddy, bug bitten, chilled, and confused—here at the doorstep of nirvana. I honestly believe that if I fully experienced how beautiful this is, I would dissolve. Poof! I can't imagine any other appropriate response. Scary, but not a bad way to go.

I'm not much for organized religion; it seems to me that it misses the point. Actually, that's what I think in my more charitable moments. Other times I think that religion is a sin which I would define as intentional separation from holiness, wholeness. If what we're looking for here is the experience of the ineffable, don't rules and structures seem a mite counterproductive? Let's put the sacred in a box with a label and instructions for operation and then it won't sneak up on us unaware and scare us to death. Personally, I'm in favor of being scared to death (says she bravely, not being faced with any imminent likelihood of same).

I'm not sure whether psychological and spiritual evolution are different layers of the same thing or only a matter of different vocabularies, but it is clear to me that they are bound up together in spite of the fact that few of my colleagues seem to be talking about this. Most clients talk "psychology" (i.e., they talk about their lives, their feelings). But occasionally someone also talks directly about her or his soul. I sometimes feel awkward and self-conscious with the words, but I appreciate it as well. It's a chance to stop for a moment and remember the heart of the matter. Remember: You are an embodiment of the divine. Or for the more concrete and literal: God loves you. Or for the psychology-minded: You are inherently worthwhile. Remember? Sometimes I make jokes: when you die and get to the pearly gates, guess what? Forget Saint Peter with his lists of crimes and accomplishments. There will be a big woman there who will ask you, "Well, honey, did you love well? Did you have fun?" What we're looking for here is joy. The real crime is in separation, in lack of love—for oneself, for other people, for nature. The patriarchy is in big trouble at the pearly gates.

Yesterday evening there was a deer in my yard. It was an adolescent—almost full grown but not quite filled out, still that auburn color. The light made the vegetation luminous, glowing. The deer shone as it munched its way around the yard, a bite here, a bite there; thick green light for dinner. I watched it eat my peas. A small sacrifice for the gift of the deer.

Pain Makes the Best Therapist

JULY 29, 1991

Not long ago, a colleague made a comment to the effect that it took a depressed mother to produce a good therapist. She was talking about how the capacity for empathy is formed. If the baby's caregiver does not meet the child's emotional needs in a reliable way, then the child is forced to reach out to the caregiver, to learn how to judge her mood. Probably an overgeneralization, of course, but one with some element of truth. I would imagine that there is some optimal level of parental failure that produces the best therapist. Too unresponsive a caregiver and the child gives up looking for what he or she needs in intimate relationships and perhaps is left too hungry to wish to form a career feeding others. But with a very responsive parent, the child has less need to focus on the caretaker, less motivation to develop the skills to elicit a response. Maybe a caregiver who is somewhat (but not hopelessly) depressed is one kind of optimal training ground for reading the nuances of another's emotional state, for developing the ability to reach out empathetically. A child hoping to know what is available from a parent who is somewhat troubled must learn intuition, must somehow make the leap of understanding that is derived from clues too subtle to articulate. But perhaps most important is the child's experience of being able to achieve understanding and connection through her or his own efforts at intuition or empathy. What a powerful feeling of satisfaction that must be. And what a powerful basis for finding that satisfaction later in life as a therapist.

This makes me think about a friend I was talking with recently. We were discussing what we've learned from living through our various family dramas. She comes from a home where there was alcohol abuse. Now she can spot an alcoholic a mile away, knows to be careful herself about drugs and drinking, and has learned (too well!) to be responsible even when those around her are not. These weren't easy lessons, but she wouldn't choose to give up the resources she's gotten from the experience.

It made me think of my own family. I got many good things as a child, things I also bring to my work as a therapist. I was treated responsibly and therefore learned to trust my judgment. I was well loved when very young, and so I feel secure in my ability to take care of myself emotionally. My parents were respectful of my privacy. Now, knowing where the line is between myself and a client comes to me effortlessly. But it may be that some of the most valuable gifts I got from my parents, at least when it comes to my ability to help others to heal, are the gifts that I paid for with scars and tears.

Bending the Rules

I wonder if other therapists do odd things in their offices now and then. Or is everyone else doing therapy by the rules? Every once in a while there's one of those points in therapy when none of the standard (or even not-so-standard) ways of working will do the trick. You can choose the best of the possibilities and be mildly ineffectual or you can get creative fast. The latter is much more fun.

My office partner and I were comparing notes recently, since we each happened to have invented an unusual response to a client that week. She had created a ritual for the easing of pain; I had intentionally stirred up a client by suggesting we not meet the following week (then waited anxiously for the client to call me and ask to have her appointment back). We each described our decision. "I did thus-and-so with this client, whaddaya think?" We each got basically the same response. "Yes, it's weird all right, but it does sound like the right thing to do."

Over the years, I've done any number of strange things in the name of therapy. Most are variations on accepted practice (accepted in some circles, anyway), although I'm sure they seem surprising at the time. Using paradox (telling someone to go home and do more of whatever the "bad" thing is), drawing rather than talking, telling stories, talking in metaphor for the whole session ("Let's not talk about you. Let's talk about your car"), getting a client to pay me for each time he or she fails to do the "homework" (and gloating to make it worse!)—I'm sure clients think I've gone off the deep end when I suggest things such as this, but they're not unheard-of. Some other methods really are unheard-of, or at least I haven't heard of them. I've been known to pick fights, read stories, send postcards, go for walks, tuck people into their chairs with blankets, write notes rather than talk, and do any number of other oddities.

Coming up with inventions such as these is great fun, although on reflection it's a bit unsettling, too. Good therapy usually means trusting my gut about what's needed. But if I'm operating in the general realm of accepted practice, I have additional reassurance that what I'm doing is right in at least some general sense. A "gut sense," after all, is useful only to the extent that a person's instincts have been shaped and informed by years of training, experience, and consultation. When I'm completely making it up, I don't have graduate school or "the literature" or my colleagues' reports to back me up; it's flying by the seat of my pants. Surprisingly, I often feel quite certain of myself in spite of that. Doing therapy is similar to playing a musical instrument: thinking well is useful but not primary. I may often play familiar melodies, but if I improvise it's still music.

The Politics of Therapy

A young man who has recently come to realize that he is gay is surprised by the amount of harassment, the level of misunderstanding and outright hatred he is experiencing. He wonders aloud to me how it was that he never noticed homophobia before. This young man is white and grew up in a family that is well-off financially. I talk to him about privilege, about how his privilege shielded him from the realities of oppression until he found himself also to be a member of an oppressed group.

A woman I see comes from a very poor family. She has managed to acquire an education, something unheard-of in the circles she comes from. Her friends are all educated and middle or upper-middle class. She feels like a fraud, an impostor. We talk about being bicultural in terms of class, and about following what is supposed to be the "American dream" and then feeling as though you've betrayed the people you came from. Another woman confesses to me the self-loathing she learned from her impoverished family, who taught her that poor equaled bad, that she should pretend to have different means, that her worth was measured by the education and income she has. She is sensitive and thoughtful enough to abhor prejudice, but she cannot seem to keep herself from feeling that poor people are not worth knowing—that perhaps she is not worth knowing.

As a feminist, I see these dilemmas primarily in terms of power and oppression. I talk with my clients about class and about homophobia. Vermont has few people of color, but I talk about racism with the white people I see, using the ways they've begun to unlearn racism as a model for how they might unlearn other destructive family or cultural messages. And of course I identify with people the aspects of their distress that are shaped by gender and its concomitant oppression and privilege: the man who has learned that need, tenderness, intimacy is dangerous; the woman who expects she deserves little, especially from men.

There is not a person on this earth whose life is not affected by oppression and privilege in some form. What the hell do nonfeminist therapists do with this dimension of human pain? Do they assume that the client is somehow responsible for feeling the way he or she does? Do they ignore it and focus on other issues? Do their clients not even talk with them about these things?

I remember hearing a gay male therapist, in a workshop about therapy with gay men, discuss the subtle ways that he knows who is an ally and what is acceptable to say. "If I walk into your office," he said, "and there are one hundred books in your bookcase and one of those books is *Lesbian Therapies,* I will see it." I recently saw a brochure put out by local social workers. On the cover was a design that showed the silhouette of a heterosexual couple. What is the message to lesbian or gay couples? What is the message to single people? Not too long ago, I propped up against my windowsill a card someone had given me that had a pink triangle (the symbol used by the Nazis to identify gays, now used proudly as a symbol of identification by lesbians and gays) and the word "ALLY" on it. One heterosexual person noticed it (a therapist I was supervising). *Every* lesbian saw it.

The power that therapists have to shape what is acceptable to speak, in what ways it is acceptable to speak, is shocking. I wonder what I may still be conveying as unacceptable? And I am frightened by what some of my colleagues may be conveying as unacceptable.

Finally Getting the Drift

NOVEMBER 12, 1991

I have mixed feelings about working with couples. It took me a while to learn that couples therapy is different from individual therapy, and I learned the hard way—by trying to work with each individual in a couples format and not having much success. But I do (usually) learn from my mistakes. I gradually developed a clearer sense of what really helps people in relationships. Now I do more playful poking at patterns, coaching change in a way that's sometimes serious but often silly. If the pair gets so conscious of patterns that they feel faintly ridiculous when continuing them, then they can try something new. I wish they'd told me in school that with couples you have to throw out 75 percent of what you do with individuals. It would have saved me a lot of time.

Now that I think of it, what may have turned the tide for me was a particular couple a number of years back. I no longer even remember what their concerns were or what patterns showed in their interactions. But I vividly recall their seeming hatred for each other, their years of grievances and resentment and anger, and my own feelings of discouragement and helplessness. It seemed that they could no longer even remember what tied them together. I worked hard and long, but with little to show for it. They couldn't separate, and they could not find a way to be together that wasn't hurtful.

I think that the experience was a shock to me, perhaps because by that time I had evolved into a reasonably skilled and successful therapist, not used to such blatant failure. I was roused to action and went to some trainings (not particularly helpful), read on the subject (ditto), thought a lot and watched my work with them carefully (both very valuable). By the time the next couple came in, I was working differently and to better effect. In fact, when I think about it, I have done reasonably well with almost every other couple I have seen since then. This isn't a cast of thousands, you understand. There has been the usual variation in (my sense of) helpfulness. But still, my feeling is that I would be pleased with each outcome in some significant way.

I'm surprised as I write this. I have thought of myself as only "adequate" with couples, told myself I didn't particularly like the work. But the truth is that I have really enjoyed every couple I have seen in the past several years. Perhaps it's time to update my self-image?

I saw a couple today (which is why I was thinking about the subject) and felt effective and excited. In considering what I liked, I told myself that this couple was "different": they clearly love each other and they are making honest efforts to describe their reality as best they can. And I imagine that this is in fact part of the picture; some couples are easier to help, for one reason or another. But I am suspicious that I have been describing every couple I've seen lately as different in some way—because they're lesbians, or because I share their political values, or because (when I need some fallback reason) I especially like them. The truth is more apt to be that *I'm* different. What a surprise. It's very likely that the impossible couple of years ago would still be difficult, and maybe I would still not be able to find a way to help them. But I wonder.

And I wonder how that couple is doing. I see one of them on the street occasionally and we say hello. She worked individually with me for a while after I stopped seeing the two of them. She made some changes that made her life more satisfying. Perhaps that changed the balance of things in the couple relationship just enough to matter. I hope so.

It's a hard thing to live with your failures. These are people's lives we're talking about here. I know that they have choices too, and that they can try another therapist or do something else to change the causes of their unhappiness. But they came to me, and I do feel a responsibility toward them. Sometimes people don't get what they want (or say they want) in therapy and it's clear to me that the responsibility is theirs, or at least shared. They may have needed to back off at a certain critical point, or needed to "prove" that no one could help, or in some deep way become caught in imagining me as their critical father or abandoning mother and been unable to break free of that. But the cases in which I know that most, or a good part, of the failure is mine—those hurt. They hurt for a long time. Wherever this couple is, I wish them well and hope that the fates have in some way brought them happiness.

ജ *1992* ഇ

Spiritual Winter

Not yet 3:00 p.m., and the sun is just down below the treeline in the west. There's a chain saw in the distance. A Vermont winter is like living in a Japanese watercolor: lots of white space and a few brush-strokes suggestive of trees. Sometimes I find the visual simplicity rest-ful, even satisfying in some deeply quiet inward way. But now, by early February, it begins to get old and boring. My body, the eternal present tense, feels locked into winter.

I'm just starting to feel better after a brief bout with a cold. I can feel the aliveness come back into my body. There is an increase in en-ergy, in possibilities, that signals health. I knew I was getting sick a couple of days ago when the speed limit seemed reasonable to me as I drove home from work. Today I knew I was on the mend when I took the stairs two at a time, my usual method. Noticing that, it occurred to me that perhaps this is how it feels for someone who's depressed and just starting to recover. It certainly matches what people have de-scribed to me.

Mercifully, I'm not very prone to depression. I've experienced the occasional "reactive depression," meaning a depression with a fairly clear precipitant, usually loss. That kind of depression generally heals itself with the passing of time and a chance to mourn, be angry, what-ever. But I've known many people who are vulnerable to a more chronic, debilitating depression, the kind that must be like always having a cold without the congestion or cough—a kind of constant lethargy in which everything takes too much effort and nothing grips your imagination or seems like fun. It doesn't take much of that be-fore it mutates into something even nastier, a discouragement that in its worst form becomes despair, an inner negativism that deepens into self-hate. What a horrible way to live. And yet people acclimate to the impossible. They live because they must, because they can't remember what it feels like to be okay, because someone has to get the kids off to school. I have watched women who were clearly so depressed that hospitalization was appropriate somehow manage to function because they had sole responsibility for their children.

When people come out of a depression like that, with the help of therapy or drugs or both, it's like waking up. They talk with amazement about starting to notice colors, or wanting to do something just for the hell of it, or actually enjoying themselves when talking to a friend. Such little, taken-for-granted aspects of life! The crime of depression is that it's so insidious; it changes everything so subtly that it may only be after the fact that one realizes what had been lost. I'm quite cheered to be bounding up the steps at my usual pace; by tomorrow, perhaps I'll feel like walking downtown to run an errand even if it could wait, or maybe I'll cruise my usual five or ten miles over the speed limit. How good it feels to have myself back. I've only been sick for three days. How must it feel to spend years with depression?

The Feminist Therapist
Diagnoses Oppression

MARCH 15, 1992

Here are her problems: She is anxious when she showers in a public place, such as the local health club. What concerns her, I wonder aloud. She keeps peering around the stall door to see if anyone is there, she says. In high school, the boys used to sneak into the girls' locker room and spy on them as they showered. Everyone knew it; no one did anything about it.

She has "problems with self-esteem." When I ask what she means, she says she doesn't speak up in meetings at her place of business, even when she has something to say. I ask her to tell me about it, and discover that the men run the meetings and take up all the air time. Several other women are there, but no woman ever speaks. Because no one has ever made a comment about this, she has assumed that it is her personal problem, a "self-esteem" problem.

She is uncomfortable working alone with men, and she wonders if she is not assertive enough. I ask her to describe her worries and learn that she has had repeated experiences of men sexualizing work situations. She is young, standardly pretty, and soft-spoken. She has rarely had a male look past that to notice whether she has anything worthwhile to say.

What shall I use as a diagnosis when I bill for this session? I need the feminist diagnosis book, which would list "oppression, gender-based" as one of my choices. Virtually all of the disabled people I have seen have used therapy as an opportunity to speak their anger at how others treat them and to puzzle out how to handle misunderstanding, ignorance, and sometimes cruelty. Every person of color I have met with talks about managing racism. This is therapy? This is consciousness raising, it's offering solidarity, it's strategizing about hate crimes. Mental illness? It's persecution.

I'm a feminist therapist, and so political action is part of my professional responsibility. I do my small bit: one more body at the rallies, speaking up when I can, political work here and there. But if the insurance companies really want to save money on psychotherapy, they should put their considerable lobbying clout behind antidiscrimination laws for lesbians and gays and sexual harassment legislation and enforcement of the Americans with Disabilities Act. They should let their employees write letters to Congress and to newspapers on company time. They should be models of gender and racial equity. Until then, I am supporting outrage, encouraging the formation of political alliances, and helping with tactics the hard way: one person at a time.

How Magic Works

I don't understand what it is exactly, that way of being that's so central to doing therapy. They sure didn't teach it to us in school. A woman I know refers to it as feeling like "a hunting dog." I know what she's talking about: that intense focus on the goal. There is indeed a feeling of straining at the leash, being almost able to *smell* the problem, the needed solution. Only I'm not following a scent. It's a feeling, an intuition, there in my belly and in the client and in the atmosphere between us. I imagine the air electric with communication. The client's words are the least of it.

One couple's problem was the husband's depression and guilt, which kept him withdrawn and his wife lonely. He'd been an alcoholic during the early years of their marriage. One night, drunk, he'd had a one-night stand with someone he'd met in a bar. This couple is deeply religious. Shocked by his behavior, the man got himself into AA (Alcoholics Anonymous) and has been sober for several years. His wife has long since forgiven him. But he still hurts daily about it, pained that he hurt the woman he loves most in the world. I had seen the couple for a while. They were doing much better, but that withdrawn depression stayed stuck. It seemed so much bigger than the crime itself. I asked whether he was ready to tackle it. His wife wondered whether he might need to forgive himself, and that made sense. So we started talking about that.

The process of this kind of therapy is subtle and quick as an otter. Under the stream of talk, I feel for the nature of his response. Does it hurt here? Is this the spot? Although something is right about this business of forgiving himself, we can both tell that it's not the crux of the matter. "Breaking my marriage vows is the most despicable thing I've ever done," he says about his infidelity. I sense substance behind that statement, the weight of judgment unleavened with mercy. He has not found a way to accept the existential frailty of being human, and human only. We talk about that and about the unremitting quality of his distress. His father cheated on his mother, he reveals. I press: *How did you make sense of that as a child?* "I saw how badly it hurt my mother and I made a solemn pledge," he says. "I would never do something like that to anyone I loved." So there it was: his infidelity was not only a matter of being unfaithful and hurtful to his wife, but also, symbolically, to his mother, and most deeply to himself. He stays depressed to punish himself for having done this "despicable thing."

I can feel him moving through the pain of recognition to a release. He is beginning to see that his mother's pain was not his responsibility, even metaphorically, and that his childhood vows can be remembered with compassion. They are separate from his betrayal of his marriage vows. That was an act he has long since atoned for. Sometime during this process his wife has taken his hand; both are weeping. I experience the echoed release in myself as well. My focus relaxes. I feel a kind of return to my usual mode of being. The hunting dog returns home. When he tells me the following week that his life feels changed in some important way, I feel pleased but not surprised.

In graduate school they taught us to see nonverbal communication and to listen for unarticulated emotion. Those are good things to know, but in retrospect they are primitive tools. There should have been a course in how to speak poetically, because powerful therapy addresses the soul, and poetry is its language. We should have studied states of consciousness and learned to change awareness and focus at will. We should have practiced naming our faults so that we would hold those of our clients with tenderness and fellowship. We should have described our mistakes to one another until we laughed, and shared our lives' secrets and stories until we cried. Oh, just let me at those beginning therapists. Have I got a curriculum for you!

A Surprise

I've been continuing this marathon sorting thing at home. Almost fifteen years of living in this house, and I feel overwhelmed with *stuff*—stuff in the basement, in closets, on shelves, in drawers. Who even knows what it all is anymore? I think years of being an impoverished student taught me to hold on to everything. I couldn't easily afford to get more, and who knew when you might need it? Now I'm feeling more settled in my middle-class status. But more deeply, it's about emotional security. I think I so profoundly felt that I alone was responsible for taking care of myself that I felt I had to hang on to any resource that came my way. Subtly, slowly, something's changed about that. I'm feeling more trusting—I guess that I can get what I need from the world, that it doesn't all have to be in my basement. All that stuff used to make me feel reassured. Now it feels constraining. So I'm sorting out, throwing away, and giving away. It feels wonderful. Every shelf or corner that I finish makes me feel lighter.

This process is striking to me because I'd been doing it for weeks before I realized what was going on. And I never would have guessed that all the clutter in my house related to all that business about self-sufficiency. I've been chipping away at that habit forever, it seems, taking little risks to be vulnerable or uncertain, to let someone be kind to me and take care of me, to not have to be so desperately okay all the time. Like tending some slow-growing plant and then waking up one morning to find that it's grown a huge flower. Oh! I had no idea!

In some ways, that's the best kind of change, I think, the one you catch yourself at. I wasn't cleaning up as an effort to do what was good for me; I was doing what I felt like doing. That's always an especially satisfying way to discover that you've really changed. It's the kind of change I love to see in clients. They look around themselves with surprise and say, "How did that happen?" There they are, living in some very different way, completely comfortable with that, and absolutely unconscious as to how it happened. That's when you know the change is real, is settled in down to your toes. You're not doing it on purpose, to look good to yourself (or your therapist). You're doing it because it's part of who you are now.

So who I am now is more open, more spacious—both emotionally and in my closets!

Working When It Hurts

JUNE 11, 1992

Rough afternoon. A close friend is moving across the country and I've been hurting about it, sometimes more, sometimes less, since I got the news a while ago. Today I made the mistake of talking with someone about it during my lunch break, and then went into my afternoon appointments all torn up inside and feeling like crying.

How am I to work? In some ways, it's not as hard as you might think to put aside my own pain and listen to that of another person. For one thing, I have to do that in smaller ways every hour that I meet with someone. There's always something of myself that could get in the way. I might be a bit hungry or tired, or have menstrual cramps, or be preoccupied with my plans for the upcoming weekend, or simply still caught up in whatever the previous client's struggle was. It's the primary act of love, I think, to set down the distorting lenses of our own needs and to see the other for who she or he really is. But it takes a significant effort of will to do that when the press of our own needs becomes larger, more insistent. It's a kind of wrenching, like trying to ignore a child who is crying himself or herself to sleep in the next room. It can be done, but not easily or lightly. In this case, I think I managed, but I noticed that I responded to my clients' pain quickly and with a little extra depth—my own pain ringing like a bell when struck by theirs.

Years ago my great aunt, whom I loved deeply, died. I remember how impossible it seemed at times to listen to clients. Especially if someone spoke of loss, I felt a rush of hurt. You can't say no to pain such as that. So the best I could do was to say, "later," promising myself that I could give the hurt attention after the day's work. And sure enough, I spent several weeks weeping in the car as I drove home, tending to that day's newly reopened wound. One thing I can say for being a therapist. It makes it hard as hell to postpone a grief process—at least for me.

A new client recently told me that she could see my pain. I don't think she meant it in any specific way, but more that she recognized me as a fellow traveler. Much of what I bring to my work is my health, a basis for my resilience and ability to stay generous, and a way to recognize the potential (and current) health in the other. But I also bring my hurt to the work. It's the foundation for any real empathy, and it keeps me from getting arrogant. I don't need to have been down the same road as the client, but I had better know something about traveling.

Ignorance

JUNE 27, 1992

Going through closet shelves in my sorting extravaganza, I came across—would you believe it?—an old reel-to-reel tape of my second-ever therapy session. It was from graduate school, my first counseling class, where we met with clients "under glass," a one-way mirror and microphone arrangement (with the professor and assorted classmates on the other side). A colleague who teaches at the local university offered to get me access to equipment that would allow me to transfer the tape onto a cassette, and I took her up on it.

What an experience to listen to that tape from almost twenty years ago. My client was an eight-year-old girl, a real scrapper, who had been through more in those eight years than I would wish on anybody in a lifetime. She told me calmly about her dad going to jail, about watching a knife fight between her mother and the mother's boyfriend. I did all right, which means I was kind and responsive and didn't make any major errors. But I sure missed a lot of opportunities. I cringed to hear myself let things go by, failures of omission. What was striking to me in listening to the tape was how obviously unskilled I sounded. I remember that at the time I was considered one of the more talented students. Whew!

I wonder how that child is today. She would be, let's see, maybe twenty-six or twenty-seven. I wonder if she likes herself as well as I liked her. I still think of her. She affected my life in an important way. I remember leaving my first session with her—my first real therapy session ever. I can still recall how stirred up I was, how amazing and complex and humbling it was to interact with another human being in that way. I wonder if she knows what she gave me by allowing me to try out my very fledgling counseling skills? I wonder if I made any difference in her life?

I just finished teaching a class for clinical psychology students. In some ways they seemed quite thoughtful and sophisticated. Did I know that much when I was in their shoes? But in many other ways, their greenness shows. I sometimes felt like their colleague, but often I felt a hundred years older. A few hundred clients older. Probably something over ten thousand therapy hours older. Old indeed.

I broached the idea of taking one of the students as an intern to my office partner, who promptly shrieked, "But they're *babies!*" Well, I suppose they are. And so was I. I have the tape to prove it.

The Delicate Balance

I was out walking early yesterday, and it seems as though the trees have started that indefinable shift of color—not to autumn's colors yet, but away from green. There's a kind of muddy cast to the leaves, an uncertainty, as if they're no longer committed wholeheartedly to summer. But the change isn't obvious either; a person couldn't tell just from looking at them what will happen, what fall looks like.

I seem to be in a similar transition. I can feel the move away from the old, the familiar, my well-known world with its comfortable edges and well-worn paths. For me, it feels like some kind of change toward being more public, an opening into a larger sphere of influence and action. But it also seems strange and uncertain. I can't tell what things will look like on the other side. I can't even quite tell what's happening. Subtle but definite, like the leaves, my change mirrors the season: a slight shift in the quality of the light, practically unnoticed and yet irrevocable.

Scary, this moving away from the known. I blithely tell my clients that there's always choice, and there is, of course. But I know more deeply that this kind of sea change, this turning, cannot really be denied, or more accurately, that the cost of denial is so high that few would willingly pay it. Even as I say that I can also feel the delicateness of the existential moment. There's a sense of being poised on the edge. It would be easy to ignore the signals, to turn around and pretend that I hadn't noticed. I could give a sigh of relief and then try to distract myself as my spirit crumbled slowly inside of me.

With clients, I often feel that combination of tenacity and fragility. I'm so conscious of the effect I have, even in slight degrees of welcome or warmth or confidence. So aware that when that new tendril appears, it is exquisitely sensitive to light, to frost. That's why I feel that the most important moments in therapy can only be trusted to my in- tuition and love, that intellect and knowledge are too clumsy as in- struments. But paradoxically, the opposite is also true. Like the tendril of ivy that pulls down the wall, there is a vigor and power to change that can't be denied any more than the tides or the seasons. I have seen people make astonishing changes in the company of therapists who are unskilled, thoughtless, and self-centered. I believe it was Ein- stein who commented to the effect that a person couldn't be a scien- tist and not come to believe in God. I don't believe in God, at least in the way people commonly think of God. But I think a person can't be a therapist without coming to experience awe, and maybe that's the same thing.

Worth a Thousand Words

NOVEMBER 14, 1992

I continue to be fascinated by hypnosis. It's really amazing to me what people can accomplish in an even mildly altered state, accomplishments that just don't feel possible to them in their everyday state. And it's astonishing how easily those resources can be accessed. It's as if someone were just managing on a limited income and then we discover loads of money in their silverware drawer in the kitchen. I always try to give people a fair amount of latitude for finding their own solutions in trance. The solutions inevitably have the accurate elegance of science and the intuitive harmony of art. People quite fluidly add whatever I've left out, change an image I suggest until it's a better fit, find words to express something with precision and grace. The unconscious is a powerful ally.

I wonder how much of the effectiveness of trance lies in my own more subtle shift in consciousness when I use it with others. In helping someone else access an altered state, I slip closer to that state myself. I imagine that my own unconscious rapport with the person and understanding of his or her needs may well be augmented as a result.

Some of the power of trance lies in the effectiveness of image as a tool, I think. One client told me about hearing her father, in a drunken rage, threaten to shoot and kill everyone in the family when he came home some night. Every night after that, she sat huddled at the top of the stairs, trying to stay awake until her father returned from the bars, prepared to waken her younger brother and get them both to safety if her father tried to make good on the threat. She was eight years old. I can see her in my mind's eye, a small, frightened, sleepy, but determined figure in her pajamas, keeping vigil. I don't think I will ever forget that image. It became a summary for me of this woman's history, her resources, and her pain. Image is the language of the unconscious, whether in or out of trance.

Another woman recently told me about a dream in which she watched in terror as a child, perched on the edge of a cliff, ignored the precariousness of her position and casually stepped off into space. A huge bird flew by and caught her softly on its back the moment she began to fall. The child giggled with delight, with no concern for how high up she was, and indeed was deposited gently on the ground moments later. I was reminded of another dream that this same person had told me some years ago. In it, she was on a train that seemed to be picking up speed as it headed inevitably for a broken bridge. She tried desperately to figure out a way to get off the train, to stop the train, all without success. They reached the bridge and saw that—surprise!—under the bridge were pillows, millions of pillows, a mountain of pillows, and with a poof! the train settled easily into their downy embrace. This woman was very surprised that I had remembered her dream from years ago, but how could I forget that image of the train? (Or the dream's message of being needlessly afraid and finding support when you least expect it. A useful reminder to all of us, myself included.)

Remarkable solutions, aren't they? Dreams so often describe the problem with uncanny precision. Advice from the unconscious, as in this woman's two dreams, is less common. In her dreams, she found resources she didn't realize she had. It is this, the hidden well of possibility, that hypnosis accesses. Hypnosis means starting from somewhere only vaguely defined and then discovering what emerges. It's like sitting on the edge of the void and dangling your feet over the brink. Remember the things that used to live under your bed when you were a kid? But in this case, the things under the bed are friendly. They have just been waiting for the invitation to lend a hand. We should remember that life does work that way, at least sometimes!

Getting Done

I seem to have finished therapy with several people over the past two or three weeks, and a couple more are planning to finish within the next week or two. That's quite an exodus at once. I wonder if it's some kind of end-of-the-year phenomenon or just coincidence. I don't remember noticing this other years, although I think there are often one or two people who, if they're about ready to end anyway, might choose the end of the year to do so in order to avoid paying another insurance deductible (which usually comes in January).

Ending therapy always evokes such a mixture of feelings for me. I feel happy, mostly, pleasure at the clients' well-being, happy *for* them as they go into their lives. Often I feel a trace of pride, too, an almost parental feeling. This person is whole and strong and I had something to do with making that happen. There's no satisfaction like it in the world, I think. At that moment, whatever cost I paid in terms of endless patience, or worry, or in struggling to find a way to be helpful, or in the pain of empathic accompaniment is forgotten, is unimportant. And part of that joy is political. Although I do other political work, I see my work with the people who come to me with their lives limited by pain one of my most valuable political contributions. Every woman who walks out of my office with greater self-respect, who can love herself in a culture that does not love women, who can make choices with a sense of personal power, is a challenge to the status quo. Every man who leaves my office able to feel more fully, to appreciate *all* of who he is, to experience intimacy, is a threat to the way things are. Inevitably, ending is a loss, too. Clients bring more than just their hurt to the relationship with me; they bring themselves. And I know I'll miss that. I'll miss this person's sense of humor, the passion for gardening I shared with someone else, another's lyrical use of language. More than the specifics, though, I'll miss the person. But mostly it's a good kind of missing. It feels right.

Less often, but still more often than I would like, the ending might also be tinged with regret. Occasionally, I can't seem to find a way to help someone. We agree that he or she should move on, but it leaves a bad taste in my mouth, that sour taste of failure, of powerlessness. Sometimes I help somewhat, but not nearly as much as I would have hoped. It may be my own limitations, or theirs, or both. But regardless of the reason, I'm saddened that we couldn't find a way together. And I always feel at least partly responsible for that.

One of my clients was talking recently about how different she felt as she was finishing therapy than the way she had expected to feel. She explained the difference by pointing to the implicit promise of "gurus" of all kinds: that once enlightened, you won't have pain, that life will be somehow easy. Her own description of how she felt was that she had become stronger and fuller inside, but that the inherent uncertainty and imperfection of life remained the same. Another woman, who was finishing therapy as a lot was going on in her relationships and in her life, spoke of how hard she was working emotionally. But, she noted, now she *could* work emotionally. She had the resources to do that and felt secure enough in herself to feel comfortable even when it was hard.

People often wonder how they'll know when they're done with therapy. It's a good question. You don't stop hurting, but the hurt doesn't run your life. You still get "caught" emotionally, but you understand it better and are on friendly terms with it. You like yourself pretty much all the time. Life has its ups and downs, but you have some tools, some skills, and most of all a sense of trust in yourself that makes it feel possible to manage whatever comes. Your feelings don't scare you. As Freud put it in defining health, you can love and work. I'd perhaps elaborate on that to say you can both give and receive love, as well as contribute to the world in some way. It's not everything, but it's enough.

ജ *1993* ൠ

A Known Evil

Two days after Inauguration Day. It's been ages since I voted for a president that won, and it's hard to get used to the idea. Maybe this is how Republicans feel! To me, politics has often been a matter of finding the least destructive candidate. Sometimes, in a local election—meaning, in a situation where it doesn't make too much difference—there's a candidate that I actually feel some kinship with. One of our senators is, I think, a genuinely good man and I usually agree with the way he votes. But it has always seemed so remote, a matter of sending in people that I hope can help control the damage done by a system that feels essentially wrong, unconnected to and even destructive of the reality of most people's lives. It reminds me that the only way I can live with the gross inequities, the cries of my fellow citizens being crushed by poverty and racism and violence, is by doing a complex combination of working for change and trying sometimes to keep the whole business out of my awareness.

I am continually struck by what human beings can live with, the level of deprivation and distress that can become the daily unremarkable givens of life. The woman who is so depressed she can barely manage, who enjoys nothing, and who lives this way for years before seeking help. The man who finds every social interaction a private terror, whose guts twist in response to a simple conversation. So many times I have asked someone about some painful aspect of his or her history, "Did you get any comfort? Did you have anyone you could talk to?" only to receive an astonished look in response. So much of what people get in therapy is simple perspective: the reactions of someone who, not having lived with whatever the client has become inured to through repetition, reacts "normally" to the telling—with horror, with anger, with empathic sorrow. A lot of how people change is by becoming resensitized, by recovering the reactions that they did not dare to have, or reactions that simply faded as the unthinkable became the expected and the expected became unnoticed.

Yet who would want to trade numbness for tears, ignorance for fury? My clients dig in their heels, not wanting to see the reality of their pain any more than I would. But I want it anyway, as do they: that unbearably painful thawing. We may take it slow, or complain all the way, or back up occasionally, but we know the direction we have to go in. What else is there to do? We may be messed up, but we aren't crazy.

Paying the Price

I am feeling very weary at the end of my day, and unaccountably sad. It's almost as if I'd like to cry but don't know why. It's the dead of winter and bitter cold. I suspect that how I feel is part cabin fever, part that I might be coming down with some bug, and part the emotional aftermath of the day.

A colleague was telling me yesterday about an article she'd seen that described "vicarious traumatization," a term for the way that witnessing the pain and hearing the stories of trauma survivors affects the helping person. This afternoon I had four appointments. Two were with people who have histories of severe abuse. One of those was having a particularly hard time today, caught between the amount of suffering that therapy seemed to "cause" by stirring up her feelings and the suffering that would obviously ensue if she did not have therapy. Both choices felt impossibly painful to her. The third client is someone whom I could only describe as distraught. She was reliving her childhood nightmare of being seven or eight years old and responsible for younger siblings in the chaotic household of alcoholic parents. My last scheduled hour was a first appointment with a woman with a fairly recent trauma. Several months ago her home was completely destroyed by flood. I began the process of detoxifying with her, which involved her telling her story carefully and with feeling. Between two of these meetings, I fielded a call from another person who was angry at me, afraid and demanding, caught in imagining that I was planning to hurt her in the way that her father hurt her so many times before.

Whew, what a day! Actually, this was just the afternoon, although the morning wasn't as tough. Vicarious trauma—I can see why I might feel a bit bruised. No matter how long I do this work, I never become immune. I imagine that I may be a little more habituated than someone who was unfamiliar with these kinds of stories, this kind of pain. But I am affected all the same.

One of the Perks

I did some self-help therapy a couple of days ago. It's good to feel some increased sense of lightness and expansiveness in that area, where I've been constricted. I'm hardly "cured," but I do have more of a feeling of possibility, partly from having a better understanding of what the trouble is and partly from some easing of what's painful about it. It was a nice bit of work.

I don't get paid vacation, and there's no pension plan, but one of the benefits of this job is that the skills I've learned are genuinely helpful in my own life. It seems to me not many occupations can boast that kind of perk. Although at times I'd prefer to remain blissfully oblivious, more often I'm grateful for the ways I've been able to enrich my life by using the things I know to assist my own psyche. Maybe I would have come to the same realizations and inner changes anyway, but it certainly seems it's been easier and maybe even quicker for me because I know something about how to help the process along. At the very least, perhaps some of the really rough spots aren't quite as unnerving because the whole arena of emotion and change is so familiar to me. All of which is definitely not to say that I always take advantage of these wonderful skills! I spend my fair share of time feeling stuck or closed down or assiduously avoiding whatever it is that's bothering me. Still, it's nice to at least have a choice in the matter.

When I think about it, it's truly disgraceful that we learn nothing about our inner selves or about how to tend to our psychological well-being. It's a sad commentary about what we consider important. Sure, people learn those skills in therapy, but it's a terribly inefficient way to educate. Most people never see a therapist anyway. They just live as best they can, with a whole aspect of their experience left vague and undeveloped and probably even a little scary. What a waste. And so the rich, living ground of inner experience gets left to the poets and the "experts," such as myself. It's ridiculous. We all know how to treat a cold or what to do for a cut or blister. Even a healthy person has an occasional bout of the flu; even a healthy person occasionally feels depressed or blocked in some way. Shouldn't all people have enough knowledge to help themselves do at least that much healing, rather than depending on distraction or the passage of time to get past the difficulty?

The Expensive Gift

The call came at 1 a.m. I am blasted awake, sounding coherent, but with a residue of confusion that follows me from sleep. *Huh? What's that ringing noise? What am I supposed to do?* It's a client's wife, saying that her husband couldn't take it anymore and wanted to go to the hospital. He won't talk to me on the phone. I say fine, take him there. She says she felt she ought to call me. I can see her point. I am the therapist, the man is in crisis and he's going to the hospital. But in fact there is nothing I can do. The call lasts no more than ten minutes, but I am awake for two hours as my body processes the adrenaline it produced.

I don't like this part of transference, the irrational belief that I somehow have magical powers to intervene when all else fails. That I can make everything okay in the face of disaster, and, furthermore, that I can do it even without the cooperation or efforts of the other person. It's partly the magical thinking of the small child who sees his or her parents as truly omnipotent. It is also partly the rage of the wronged person who wants to even the score with his or her parents by hurting them back, making them feel just as trapped, equally powerless. Only, of course, they aren't calling their parents at 1 a.m. They're calling me.

I seem to have had a couple of these lately: an adult sounding for all the world like a sophisticated version of a hostile teenager, daring me to try to fix it. "I'm suicidal and I refuse to go to the hospital and I will not promise you that I will keep myself safe. What are you going to do about it?" What indeed? If I force hospitalization, I betray the client; if I do not and the person harms himself or herself, I am professionally and morally liable. I am guaranteed a struggle, because that's what the person needed to do with his or her parents. Aha! I caught you doing it wrong! Now I'm positive that your caring has been a sham. You don't really understand me. I'm not important to you. Prove that you love me. And underneath it all the desperate wailing hope of the injured child that perhaps, just maybe, finally, someone will come through for him or her. Except that it's far too terrifying for this person to allow that.

I suppose it's the lot of the therapist to remain unseen in certain ways, and to be unseen *and* punished for the other's distortion is frustrating at best. But even as I want to yell at the person to "get a grip!" I can recognize the possibilities for something good. There's a huge potential for transformation in the context of crisis. I have seen people change their lives based on the outcome of a crisis. It is unparalleled as an opportunity for learning.

I know people who have skated right up to the edge—of suicide, of relapsing into alcoholism—and discovered definitively for the first time that they valued themselves too much to destroy their lives. This information could only be had, for them, by peering into the abyss. I know couples who have used an affair or the decision of one person to move out, events that usually tear a relationship apart, as a fulcrum for change, an opening to a deeper commitment. A crisis can show you what you really want. If you don't let the pain and fear paralyze you, you can reach beyond your old assumptions and limits to something truly new.

I took part in an art therapy exercise once. The facilitator brought in a wonderful assortment of stuff: long spools of paper, yarn, feathers, balloons, markers, cardboard. We were instructed to make anything we wanted. Anything. We could use *all* the stuff. I experienced something close to an ecstatic state for the next chunk of time, which might have been half an hour or two hours, I couldn't say. The aftermath of a crisis is like that. We have so much! We can use it to make whatever we need to; it's all right there, rich and complicated and easily available. I'm so glad, afterward, that the crisis has occurred, so grateful for what it has yielded and for the opportunity to help make something out of it. If only it could happen without the make-the-therapist-pay phase!

Up from the Ashes

JUNE 1, 1993

After all this time, she still walks into my office with her eyes averted, as if looking about in a strange place, drawing my attention away from herself. It's a good metaphor, that entrance, for this is someone for whom the world itself is a strange place. So much has been written about the consequences of abuse, and they are indeed great. But I continue to be thunderstruck by the effects of neglect, the unspoken damage.

Once we started to talk about it, she described herself as having "never moved out of the college dorm." It's an apt description. I hadn't even thought to ask, and she hadn't thought to remark, and so it was all the more striking as the details started to emerge. These aren't exactly your standard intake questions. "Do you know how to do laundry?" "Can you make yourself supper?" This is someone who did not know how to put herself to bed, did not know how to grocery shop or fix herself regular meals, and had little furniture in her home. In fact, she was living pretty much the way you would expect a child to live who had been suddenly abandoned by her or his parents.

Many clients have told me that between abuse and neglect, they prefer abuse. At least it's a form of connection. Neglect runs deeper, cutting at what it means to be human. Abuse is a betrayal of relationship. Neglect is an absence of relationship.

I have heard stories of people who had to be instructed by the school nurse about the necessity of brushing their teeth or bathing regularly. I recall a woman telling me that she learned from her college roommate how to wash dishes and clean a room. I don't think the roommate even knew what she was teaching; my client simply watched hungrily and covertly. This is someone who now always looks beautifully put together. You would never imagine that she grew up so completely untended. Another client, as a child, managed to show up at her neighbor's home around suppertime every day. That way, she knew she'd get fed. Astonishingly, these were generally not situations of parents who were alcoholics or seriously mentally ill or even single parents. They were more often simply parents who were overwhelmed; who, having lived through similar neglect, knew little about making a home; who felt hopeless or who were self-centered. They were mothers who were drowning in depression and fathers who were self-absorbed and saw childrearing as the woman's responsibility.

My client who still "lives in the dorm" is trying to learn what normal is—not the normal of prescribed behavior, but the normal of having a predictable life that makes for some kind of ground under her feet, of having a home instead of a dorm room. She practices going to bed at night. She tries to remember to keep food in the house. Her current challenge is to do the laundry regularly and actually put the clothes away instead of selecting the day's outfit from the pile on the floor. Yet this is someone who does a fine job at work, who has friends, and who has a deep connection to her church. She has a gentle good-will and an ability to laugh at herself that attracts people. Sitting with her, I feel a combination of maternal bossiness ("Did you do the laundry this week?") and awe. How amazing, this ability to create a meaningful life around crushing barriers. Someone yesterday asked me whether she can ever hope to feel better, given how awful she feels now and how far back into her history that awful feeling reaches. I thought of this woman who is teaching herself to have a home and said, "Absolutely."

It's for You

I've had more than the usual amount of crisis calls lately. It's odd, the way they sometimes seem to come in batches. I have no idea what to attribute that to. It's summer, when people usually feel better. It isn't the full moon. Maybe it's not environmental at all. Maybe it's just random distribution, like a coin coming up heads several times in a row.

When I worked at a mental health center, we used to rotate being on call. How I dreaded that. The calls came from people I didn't know at all, had no relationship with, had no sense of context for their distress. I had no way to judge whether I could trust them to do what they agreed to do, no way to weigh the seriousness of the problem except by the information in front of me at the moment. We were given this responsibility with no training. It was assumed that all mental health professionals were automatically competent for the job. I remember jumping when the phone rang, my heart pounding in the middle of the night, impossible to get back to sleep after a late call.

It's a very different matter to get a call from one of "my" clients. I know which person has feelings that gallop away with him or her and thus may just need help getting perspective, and who minimizes so much that any call must be considered a very serious matter. I have a relationship with the caller that I can depend on. I can generally trust the person to tell me the truth, to follow through on what we plan, and if I can't expect that I usually know it.

But more important, these are people I care about. I *want* them to call me if they truly need to. I'm committed to them, to their struggles, to their well-being. I think, for example, of one woman who called me recently. This woman lived through betrayal and assault at the hands of her mother, the person who theoretically was assigned to protect and nurture her. Her father escaped to his office, choosing not to know what was going on. In her life, her only dependable friend when in deep pain has been the bottle. She learned early that humans were not interested in her suffering. Now she is no longer drinking. A call to me when she cannot endure her injury is an act of courage, a revolution. We should dance in the streets. I mean it when I tell her that I am glad she called.

But people's timing isn't always convenient. My clients can hardly be expected to know that three other people have called me with an emergency this week. Nor should that matter, anyway. It's the same dilemma as with therapy, writ large. What each person deserves is nothing less than the best I have to offer: my fullest attention, my most warmly responsive caring, the greatest skill and thoughtfulness I possess. What they get instead is sometimes shaded with weariness, resentment, or frustration. It's easier to put aside my preoccupations and needs when I have an appointment and so have prepared room in which to welcome the other. But as with an unexpected guest, even one that I want to see, it's more difficult when I am involved in something else, or thought I'd have the time to myself, or am pulled out of a "now I get to collapse" mind-set. At those moments, I feel as though I just can't bear to take care of one more person for one more minute.

With extremely rare exceptions, my clients are more than respectful of my personal time. Usually, I encourage them to call when they need to. I know the significance of that gesture and want to give that. So we navigate as best we can between the opposing needs: theirs to be able to ask for my response when it matters, and mine for the privacy and renewal of a life separate from my work.

Pissed Off

AUGUST 22, 1993

It is Sunday evening and I've had an hour or two in which to renew myself enough to bring myself fully to my work. Things seem to have eased slightly, but the level of client need I'm responding to is still at an unprecedented pitch. There's been an unfortunate convergence in my life of a long stretch of family visits along with what would be impossible work demands even under the best of circumstances. It makes me wonder if I should move somewhere less attractive to visitors. Iceland, perhaps.

The big family barbecue was a few days ago. In the middle of it I got a call from a client saying that she had made a suicide gesture. She was, thankfully, out of medical danger and was being carefully watched by family and friends. But she was furious with all of us for not somehow making her pain go away and was using her rage to hurt those around her. I, as well as her family, felt helpless and exasperated and angry at being put in a position of responsibility for her well-being with not a thing I could do about it. She refused to agree not to harm herself. She refused to go into the hospital. She had put all of us in a bad spot, and her tone of voice said that she knew it.

It happens rarely, but one of the hardest moments in being a therapist is when you lose your therapeutic stance, lose that feeling of warm generosity that is detached enough to allow you to let go of outcome and concentrate on the lived pain and possibility in the person before you. Without it, I'm of no more help than the frustrated friend or the distancing spouse. I was pissed off at this client, I knew it, and I knew further that I was worthless as her therapist unless I found a way to feel differently. I've only had a few clients who have put me in this kind of bind, but every time it's been awful. I hated feeling helpless. I needed a relationship to her and to her pain that was both accepting and challenging without feeling personally entangled, and I didn't have it. I told a few people the barest outline and got murmured sympathy. I was angry for a while, then tried (with only marginal success) to let go of it. Then it was late and I went to bed.

I awoke with the solution, a way to approach her, a place to stand. Her behavior, after all, was information, information that might under normal circumstances take ages to get at in therapy, especially considering that when not under duress, this was a pretty well-protected person. I knew she was committed to her therapy. I guessed that if I approached her with kind curiosity, she would be able to search with me for the clues inherent in what was, after all, not very reasonable behavior. Sure enough, as we probed it became clear that what she did made perfect sense in the context of her life as a child. She was abused regularly and her caregivers did nothing to stop the pain. It was in their power to respond. Her well-being was their responsibility and yet they let her suffer. It must have been a horrifying glimpse of the worst of human nature. How could they allow her to be so hurt? Surely if they knew how awful she felt they would stop it.

If she could have dared then, she would have been furious. Now she was an adult and she could risk finally expressing that. And she wanted us to know just how she felt: powerless and enraged. She wanted us to know that in the deepest and most immediate way possible: by feeling it ourselves. Because if we knew, if we really understood how badly she hurt, wouldn't we find a way to stop her pain?

None of this was intentional, of course. She didn't lie awake plotting how to make the people who cared about her feel the way she felt as a child. She wasn't thinking, "Oh, this is just like when I was abused." The psyche is a mysterious thing and has its own knowledge, its own reasons, its own logic.

By some strange coincidence, I was told yesterday of an incident between someone in my family and her teenage daughter. The witnesses were horrified but followed the great dictum of noninterference in the family matters of others. I, the family psychologist, heard it as emotional abuse. How can I not interfere when I have seen, over and over, the enormously destructive consequences of noninterference? The pain of so many people is based not only on the harm done immediately to them but also, more deeply, on the harm done by those who knew and chose to remain silent. How can anyone feel trust in a human world that will stand by in silence as you are being tortured?

I have decided to write a letter to this family member and tell her the story I heard and the concerns I have. I will need to approach this thoughtfully; she carries her own pain, which of course is the source of the hurt she inflicts on her children. But, as with my client who could express what she needed to with remarkable precision as she remained completely unaware of her motives, this woman has no wish to damage her children. She thinks only of her authority and the imagined necessity of enforcing obedience. I will approach her as kindly and clearly as I am able. I hope that she will find a way to allow her love for her child to be larger than her need to feel powerful. Then I, at least, will be able to look at myself in the mirror without reproach.

Trusting the Experts

The sky today is a smorgasbord in gray, as it often is in November: pearl gray, lead gray, gray soft as a bird's feather, cold as a closed door. November has a quality of time suspended, the wait for winter. It's unusually mild today. I went outside to lie down briefly and admire the layers of color in the landscape. It is easier for me to do in my current state, which is recovering from yesterday's illness. Nothing like being sick to slow down the body wonderfully.

My illness was probably a reaction to the herbs I'd just started to take in an effort to do something about large uterine fibroids. When my fibroids were diagnosed, it became clear that all that Western medicine could offer was surgery if and when it becomes necessary. Not liking to be so helpless, I consulted a naturopath, who prescribed the regime of herbs responsible for yesterday's illness. Family members, when they heard of this development, immediately asked what I knew about the naturopath, how I could know if the herbs were really okay to take. Well, they're right. How do I know if this person is a fraud, if she's ever had any success with fibroids, if these herbs are toxic? How do I know the same about my physician, for that matter? When I consult individuals with expertise, I put myself in their hands to some extent, trust that they know their business.

A close friend who's having trouble in her primary relationship has been seeing a couples therapist. It's obvious that all hell has broken loose with this couple since they started therapy. Some of that, at least, has to do with the way the therapist has defined the couple's problem, a definition that makes my friend look "guilty" and takes the focus off her partner.

It's hard to know what to think. With the naturopath, I partly want to believe her explanation that I must be allergic to one of the herbs. Another part of me questions whether it's wise to believe her at all and never wants to take any herb again as long as I live. And who knows about my friend's therapist? Maybe things getting worse is exactly what this couple needs. Lord knows they've been treading water with this problem long enough. But maybe this relationship will be torn apart, and torn apart needlessly, because of ill-informed therapeutic interventions.

It makes me think about my own effect on people, of course. I reassure my supervisees and myself that our clients are active participants, that people ignore their therapists all the time, that they are perfectly capable of taking what's helpful and throwing out the rest. But I know that it's not quite as easy and guilt-free as that. I'm (we're) not off the hook quite that easily. People consult me because they assume I have certain expertise. If they can't rely on that expertise at least somewhat, why bother? I blithely assume my expertise as well, move confidently through the territory of people's emotions and pain and dreams, as if I had every right in the world to apply my judgment to their lives. I know that they invite me, and I know that I do what I can to help them judge for themselves too. More to the point, I know that I will be unable to work at all if I feel my responsibility too heavily. But just the same, at least today, I can't quite reassure myself out of the terror of that weight either.

Living Outside the Lines

I started a juice fast three days ago. I just couldn't bring myself to try those herbs again; they feel like poison to me. Now they're compost. Anyway, a two-week juice fast was the alternative treatment for fibroids suggested by the naturopath. I feel fine physically. But it's been amazing to me how difficult it's been psychologically. I'm scared, is what it comes down to. I feel as though I'm off in uncharted territory, adrift and alone.

Some of it is simple unfamiliarity and lack of support. I feel as though I am the weirdest person in the world. Although my friends are trying to be supportive, the operative word here is "trying." With two exceptions, the universal reaction I've gotten is some version of being aghast. The exceptions, interestingly enough, are both people who have lived a fair amount of time in California. One is a friend whose reaction was clearly positive, the other a family member who had a friendly, nonchalant, "that's interesting" kind of response. In California, which a colleague recently referred to as "the altered state," a fast is only one of any number of interesting and alternative things that lots of people are doing. Here in the Northeast, I don't know a soul who's been on a two-week fast.

The other scary thing is something more primitive. Eating is so basic, such a given in my life and the lives of everyone I know. Can you really separate eating and life like this? I know I can skip a meal, even stop eating for a couple of days. The body is resilient. It can manage without food or sleep or whatever for a little while. I know that physically, kinesthetically. But *two weeks?* I can't even imagine it. My body knows nothing about that, nothing about continuing to live, nothing about feeling all right, in the context of no food. Fasting for three or four days feels within my ken. But seven days? Ten? *Fourteen?* This must be how an alcoholic feels; I can only imagine continuing with the fast today, noticing that I feel all right, and refuse to think any further.

It makes me think of the kind of existential terror that people often feel in therapy when making those deepest changes in character. There's a moment (although in reality that moment may last weeks) in which you have leapt off the cliff, and like a cartoon character, hang suspended in space, feeling the irrevocability of your decision and the absolute knowledge that everything in your experience predicts your destruction. There's no help for it. I can tell the other person that I've seen this before, that I know she or he will make it, but in truth I haven't seen *that* person do this particular leap before. I'm an outside observer. It's easy for me to say (as they often remind me!). I've found a book about fasting that was enormously reassuring. But that's about other people's experiences, not mine. I can only live it, listen to my body as best I can, and learn that, like my clients, I survive.

so *1994* cs

Nowhere to Hide

JANUARY 27, 1994

The local library has yet to be computerized. When I take a book out, I simply bring it to the counter and chat with the librarian while she stamps it. There are no library cards. I don't even have to say my name. They know who I am. At the bookstore I once was asked for a deposit to order a book. A longtime employee standing nearby smiled at the new employee who had made the mistake and waved me out. The bookstore doesn't need to ask me for deposits. The employees know who I am. When my partner went to a nearby clothing store to find a birthday present for me one year, the clerk, on discovering who the gift was for, said, "Oh, I know who she is. I've heard wonderful things about her. I'll help you find something nice." The people in the hardware store in town have a habit of knocking a little something off the price when I make purchases. I think they do that with almost everyone—that is, with everyone who looks familiar to them. I don't recall that I got these discounts fifteen or twenty years ago, when I was relatively new in town.

Much as I complain about the lack of privacy that is the inevitable consequence of living and working in a rural area, there is also something enormously comforting about being known and recognized. I sometimes fantasize about what a relief the anonymity of an urban setting would be, but I imagine that it would feel isolating and lonely as well. Here in small-town America, you can't get away from your past. That can be suffocating for anyone and especially discouraging for someone trying to make any significant change. But it also can be reassuring in an odd way. None of us can get away with being too slick. We all bring our histories like a ragtag entourage wherever we go in our little small-town world. Sometimes that means that we are petty, refusing to accept someone's present capabilities because we recall his or her earlier indiscretions. But I think it can also mean that we have a particularly humane and forgiving perspective. We have to live with ourselves and with one another, flaws and all. We can't easily afford to avoid or ignore or hate too many people. There just aren't enough other resources to substitute. We have to come to terms with some essentials of human nature, including our own, whether we like it or not. There's really nowhere to hide, after all.

It's such a gift, and it's scary, this business of being known. I see it in my clients and in myself with my friendships. My clients watch me to discover how accurately I will see them and what my response will be to that seeing. They struggle variously to show me who they are, longing for company, and to disguise their reality, terrified at recognition. With my friends, I have known both sides. Nothing compares with the relief, the comfort, of being really known, of having a fellow traveler look into my eyes, see me, and respond with welcome. And there is little worse than pain inflicted by someone who knows me well, someone who can hurt me because of that knowing.

I once consulted with a college teacher who was concerned about one of her students. She had a large office with a number of chairs. We sat near each other at one end of the room. During the course of our conversation, she got up to sit elsewhere several times, each time moving farther away from me. By the end of the time, we were sitting at opposite ends of the room. I got the distinct impression that the more helpful and insightful I was about the student, the greater her fear that I would see her too. I am reminded of the observation that language is a device invented by man to conceal his thoughts. I suppose all relationships are a matter of the delicate tension between concealing and revealing. The cost of being seen can be high, but the cost of staying hidden is unbearable.

A Slump

I seem to be doing uninspired work lately, just plodding through my days. I'm attentive and, I think, effective enough, but not passionate. It's feeling more like just a job. I do it reasonably well, and that's that. Could be that I need a vacation. Or maybe it's just another symptom of late-winter cabin fever or some kind of middle-aged therapist phenomenon. I've been doing this work for twenty years now. It would stand to reason that my feelings might shift in that period of time.

I recently paid too much for Carl Goldberg's *The Seasoned Psychotherapist,* hoping to find some perspective. Unfortunately, the author's biases toward focusing on the experience of male analysts shows through all too clearly, so the book's relevance to me feels limited. I would have asked different questions, I think. How has doing psychotherapy for all these years changed the way that you see human nature? How has it influenced your spirituality? What has it cost you emotionally? Knowing what you do now, would you choose differently?

A very expensive profession, psychotherapy. Emotionally it has cost me dearly: in echoed heartache, in secondhand images of cruelty and suffering. But if psychotherapy has cost me the innocence of not knowing, it has also given me the keys to transformation. It has been for me a form of spiritual practice. Knowing what I do now, I still can't imagine choosing anything else for work.

The Curative Powers of May

MAY 24, 1994

I've recently returned from a few days away to discover that all of Vermont has exploded into spring. Everything is astonishingly, achingly lush, almost tropical in its impact, but lighter, lighter—in color, in the feel of the air. A walk through downtown is ambrosia, so intensely sweet with birdsong and scented air and color that it feels as though it can't be real. Perhaps it's at least illegal? Banned: walking outside from mid-May to mid-June. Produces intoxication over the legal limit. At home, the countryside is without the borders and confines of civilization, and the green stretches on in gleeful triumph. "Ha!" It screams, "Life, life, life, *life!*"

Could someone remind me why I'm doing therapy? People do seem to feel better in the summer. It's amazing how many of them keep their appointments faithfully. Mostly I just do the work (a feat made possible by the fact that my office is indoors), but sometimes the whole thing strikes me as crazy. Excuse me, you feel *depressed?!* Have you looked outside lately? Let's stop this silly talking and go for a walk or dig in the ground. What's happening outside is far more therapeutic than anything I could possibly hope to conjure up.

Come to think of it, what am I doing sitting inside writing?

Hear What I Do, Not What I Say

I've had a couple of occasions lately to be reminded that people's pain is sometimes better expressed in how they are than in what they say. I have a relatively new client, a woman, who certainly has plenty in her life to cause her distress. Yet this is someone with a lot of resources, both personally and situationally. How is it that she has stayed "stuck" in this painful position for so many years? I probed tentatively for what about *her,* about how she understood and lived her life, might be contributing to her distress. No luck. In fact, every time she would make a comment that might suggest what the trouble was, and I would ask her about it, she would tell me that it didn't seem quite like that to her. Finally, I realized that this pattern itself was her way of expressing something about where she hurt. This is someone who was always "wrong" as a child, always criticized. How could she even begin to think about herself as part of the problem without feeling devastated, without that old feeling of being wrong? Oh! Well, it took me a few sessions of bumbling around. But now I have a clearer sense of where it hurts, and most important, how to proceed without reinjuring her. In some ways, I'm glad for her stubborn refusal to allow me to intervene in ways that didn't help or may have made it worse.

With someone else, our struggle has been mostly in the area of limits. I haven't talked to her about this yet, so I don't know what she will be able to tell me about it. But I do notice that she has had serious difficulty with every limit I have set: time of session, length of session, cancellation policy, and so forth. We have had extended discussions about these and other practical matters of therapy. When I don't agree to what she wants, she is angry and experiences me as cold and withholding. Here, my self-knowledge is critically valuable to me as a way to judge what she is saying. I know myself and others' reactions to me well enough to know that others do not generally see me this way. I wonder what this means to her. Does she feel so young and hungry inside, and so unable to ask for nurturing, that she can only express her need by trying to get me to make "special arrangements" for her? This is someone with a lot of experience in therapy. Presumably, she knows the standard limits of the therapeutic contract. Is she asking for exactly what she knows I cannot give so that she can replay with me a familiar relationship, that of a cold withholding parent, for example? Is she trying to find out if I am strong enough to stand my ground, clear and experienced enough to keep the framework of therapy solid for her, and personally secure enough to withstand her anger? Perhaps it's all of these.

I remember in graduate school we did an exercise in which we adjusted a tape recorder so that we could hear the voices of the people talking but not the words. The task was to understand what was going on without being distracted by the content, the stories. What a person says is important, but so is how she or he says it. But in addition to both of those things, I try to attend to the subtle and complex way that a client steers me in a particular direction, the way she or he habitually reacts to my comments, the things assumed about me or about therapy. What if he or she contradicts everything I say? It's information, I might guess, about some injury in the area of trust and safety. It's a way of telling me, "I have to be completely in charge or something terrible will happen. I know it. No one besides me has ever really had my best interests at heart." If the client changes the subject every time I ask about feelings, maybe he or she is scared to feel, or maybe doesn't even know how. If the client passively waits for me to tell her or him what to do, what does this tell me about how powerless she or he feels or about the client's history of being bossed around? All of those things, and more, point inevitably to the person's image of the world: the assumptions about what is possible between people, about who he or she is, about what can and cannot be said.

We each carry such a map of the world in our psyches. The map may say that no one can really be trusted, that you will only be loved for what you can give, or any of a million hurtful and limiting rules.

Usually those rules were learned in pain and in terror by someone too young to have any perspective or even awareness of what the rules meant. What mattered is that at the time, the rules helped him or her to avoid some of the hurt. Now, decades later, I look at someone in distress and try to discover what those rules might be. It's hard. The client, of course, has no way to tell me directly. This map by definition is made up of the things that are never questioned, the "givens," the ways of being that are in her or his bones. I can only try to look underneath what is taken for granted and in the spaces between what he or she and I say or do, hoping for a clue.

The War Against Women

She's a writer, and in the story she showed me, a woman is living in some kind of collective or community in which the men assume an absolute sense of entitlement and ownership over the women and children. She is one of the lucky ones whose man treats her well and has not been abusive to her in any way—so far. She watches the other women, looks into the eyes of those who have given up, who no longer even think about injustice or imagine escape. She sees their false smiles, their compliance. She plans her escape and waits for an opening. In the meantime, she witnesses a man forcing sex on another woman and is powerless to intervene. No woman dares to name the crime. No man considers that this event is anything other than normal, ordinary.

"This story is my life," she says. Not just her life, but women's lives and their reality. The story captures starkly, as tales do, something of Truth. The writer is a woman who has lived a version of this reality. She knows that it is a reality shared by other women as well.

I live a privileged life. I have an education, a job that enables me to support myself economically, a partner who is loving and responsive. I have choices, the essence of privilege. Yet I recognize myself in her story; I know she speaks for me and for other women who have resources as well as for those who do not. The reality this chronicle portrays is ugly and frightening. Much of the time I don't think about it. I live in my comfortable home and go to my comfortable job and generally do more or less as I please. But the truth is that underneath my general experience of safety and freedom, a small, alert part of me always feels a bit afraid, a little cautious. I react differently when I hear a man's footsteps behind me, an unknown man's voice on the phone, when I see that it is a man who is at my door or has come to fix the furnace, differently than if the footsteps, the voice, the visitor were female. Like all women, I make slight adjustments every day to protect myself—adjustments that I do unconsciously, decisions that no longer even feel like limitations because they are so much a part of how I live, how all women live.

I remember vividly the first all-women's conference I went to. It was sometime in the early 1970s. I was astonished by how I felt: energetic, expansive, almost giddy with a sense of aliveness. I asked myself why, and the insight that followed remains one of the most important of my life. It was because that was the first time that I was in a situation where I felt truly safe from men. And so by putting down for that brief time the weight of always being a little afraid and constrained, I learned finally what that fear and constraint cost me. I want to emphasize again that I am one of the lucky ones. I have had my share of harassment, of the mundane reminders of my precarious position as a woman, but I have not been raped or battered. The burden that I carry is one of the lightest, only the minimum.

As others have said, there is a war against women. Most of the time I don't think about it, even as I help to bandage the casualties in my office. If I really thought about it, how could I live? I imagine that men, who aren't forced to notice it in the way that women are, think about this war even less frequently than I do. I'm talking about the enlightened men, of course. I assume that most men would argue that there is no war, that I'm overdramatizing. They would argue this in spite of the statistics on all forms of violence against women, statistics far more dramatic than those of any "real" war (i.e., war primarily among men). I wonder what would have happened had my client brought her story to a male therapist—even to an enlightened male therapist?

Soul-Searching

Supervising other therapists is such an odd undertaking. It's not like what one might normally think of as what a supervisor does, i.e., look over the person's work and approve or give suggestions for change, although that's certainly part of it. The instrument of change in therapy is the person of the therapist. So even though supervision must attend to matters of technique and understanding, it must also look at the therapist himself or herself. It's a tricky balance, because looking at the psyche of the other begins to shade over into therapy. I have learned (the hard way, by making mistakes at it) that therapy in the context of supervision is confusing and not necessarily helpful. Yet to ignore the ways in which the therapist's own blind spots get in the way of his or her work is to miss one of the most important aspects of the therapy. This would not be good supervision either.

So I tread delicately around the edges of my supervisees' hurts, trying to point out how those hurts influence their work, hoping to offer some clarity and compassion about what is going on without crossing that uncertain line into actually doing therapy with the person.

Privilege influences therapists' work, too. It's all too natural for a therapist to be frustrated or confused when a client has trouble in some area of life that has always been easy for the therapist. If you have never had to struggle with standing up for yourself or knowing what you want, it can be mysterious and annoying when your client doesn't even know where to start.

Sometimes it's fairly easy. I'm thinking of one man I supervise who gets repeatedly caught in feeling insecure about his work, and then is oversensitive and handles it badly when challenged by a client. He's a relatively new therapist and feeling successful matters significantly to him. Sometimes, without even noticing, he communicates to clients in subtle ways the importance that they appreciate him, that they feel he is doing good work with them. Not much room for a client to be angry, to be disappointed in the therapy or the therapist. And certainly it's not fair that the client be asked to take care of the therapist in this (or any) way. In this case, the therapist and I were able to notice together what he was doing and to explore a bit about what that meant in his life. Why was being reassured in that way so critical to him? What would it mean for him to do without that reassurance? We talked also about how the problem tended to show up in his work. We considered the warning signs, both inside him, the therapist, and in the client, that might indicate that he was getting caught in this way. We discussed the ways in which his work suffered as a result. In this case, we were able to be allied and sympathetic enough to make it possible for the therapist to look without shame at his own failings. While therapeutic, I'm sure, it wasn't quite the same as therapy. We identified the trouble but didn't try to change it. The change is up to the therapist to accomplish in whatever way he can.

But this was an ideal scenario. Things don't always work out quite so cleanly. I recall a supervision session recently in which the therapist, her own pain stirred up by recognizing the ways she was being controlling with her clients, burst into tears in our supervision meeting. What then? Explore dispassionately the causes of her distress? Hardly appropriate. When somebody bleeds, you administer first aid. The time to figure out what happened is later.

Talking about one's work as a therapist is serious soul-searching. It's not easy and it's occasionally painful. It takes a real commitment to one's work and the people one works with to be willing to poke around in the recesses of one's psyche that way. In fact, to manage that kind of self-examination in any reasonable way, one has to become extremely good at self-forgiveness, at patience with one's failings. It feels bad to know that someone you care about (i.e., the client you're discussing) is getting less than the best possible help because of your personal limitations. Yet the only way for that client to get good help is to look openly at yourself as well as at the client. It takes courage to be a therapist, although not in the way that people often think. Sometimes someone will comment to me that it must be hard to hear the stories of how others were hurt. It's true that that can be enormously difficult. But what takes courage as a therapist is not so much listening to the pain of others as listening to your own pain.

Emotional Whiplash

AUGUST 3, 1994

Well, I have emotional whiplash. I met with a woman who at eleven was abandoned by her only parent, her mother. Much of her struggle with me has been about trust. Lately, she has been increasingly frightened about how close she's getting to me. In her world, that can mean only danger. She knows in her belly and heart that love only brings pain. The tension between us has been palpable. I've been doing my best to hold my ground and stay open and emotionally connected to her, hoping that time and experience would help. Then, today, she fired me. She had the courage to come tell me why. How could she trust me when I was taking care of her for money? It was inevitable that I would dump her in the same way that her mother dumped her. She "threw her away" to the care of an alcoholic and indifferent aunt when my client's existence was an obstacle to a marriage with a wealthy man. My client was sure, therefore, that the fee she paid me mattered more to me than she did, just as her own mother had chosen money over her daughter. Trembling, angry, crying, she refused referral to another therapist, saying that she'd been a fool to trust me as much as she had. She thought the best she could hope for was to close down her feelings and somehow try to survive.

It was so obvious to me that nothing I said would make the slightest bit of difference to her at that point. I could understand and sympathize as well as I could manage. I could try to tell her what I thought was going on between us. But for her there was only one reality at that moment: her terror at how she *knew* I would betray her trust. I could only let her go, all the while frightened myself for her well-being, knowing that the possibility of her choosing suicide as a way out of her pain was as real as it had ever been in our time together. Was there something else I could have done? Some way to have prevented this? Would she be okay? How long would it take her to understand what had happened? Could she let herself call me once she did? Since she left the session early, I had some time to agonize. Then my next appointment started.

My next client was someone I'd been meeting with for only a couple of months, but who has made almost unbelievable changes in that period of time. She had come to me so flooded with anxiety and self-hate that she had been unable to take care of her toddler, and had frequently collapsed into tears at her part-time job. During our first sessions, she shook and wept uncontrollably. For this woman, gaining an understanding of why she was so anxious and nonfunctional was like opening a door. Now she could see herself with compassion, and that in turn allowed her to choose other ways of responding. She flew ahead like a bird released from a cage. Over the next few weeks, I saw her move with dizzying speed into a comfortable sense of herself as capable and happy. I mostly sat back and watched and applauded. Today she came in to report her newest successes. She herself was amazed at how differently she felt. In the middle of the session, moved by gratitude toward me for my part in these changes, she leapt up out of her seat and hugged me. Well!

It feels so odd to be the recipient of such powerful emotional reactions and yet to know that they have very little to do with me personally. The woman who fired me was firing her mother, not me. I'm sure I've made mistakes with her, but I have been, and continue to be, trustworthy. The woman who hugged me was responding partly to my help, but I would be arrogant to think that her changes were mostly my doing. A person who teaches a child to read can hardly consider herself or himself responsible for that child's production of a prize-winning novel years later.

In a postscript, the woman who fired me called me later that week. She was still fuzzy about what had happened, but knew that ending our relationship was a terrible mistake. That phone call was perhaps one of the braver things she's done. Still inevitably expecting betrayal, she was astonished when I welcomed her back with concern and relief and warmth. The woman who hugged me decided with pride and only a touch of worry that she could risk having less frequent appointments. I collected my things and headed home, contemplating the vicissitudes of the human heart.

It Takes Guts

I saw a woman yesterday for a brief series of sessions using a new technique I learned to help her with some trauma symptoms. It's stressful to do that kind of intense work with a client with whom I had no prior relationship. I worked extra hard to make sure I had her non-verbal signals right, trying to help her feel safe enough to do what she needed. The technique itself tends to elicit powerful responses, and the client alternately dissociated, experienced dry heaves, had trouble breathing, cried, and trembled. My job was to be as sensitive as I could to what she needed and how to support her, to use this technique with skill, and most important to contain this flood of feeling.

At the end of the session the client said she felt flattened, exhausted. I knew what she meant. It costs, keeping company with that level of horror. It really is an unnatural act, I suppose, to stay emotionally present and responsive to pain. As I see in my clients and know in myself, the natural reaction is to flee, strike out, or to make it stop or to get away. A person must be a little crazy to invite the expression of pain and then to stay and look it in the eye.

And what of this client's ability to stay with the pain, for that matter? Oh, I was brave and strong and all that, but *she* was astonishing. Over and over she was pounded with emotion. I watched her face for permission, or asked, "Can you go on?" and each time, through the tears or the headache or the nightmare image, she chose to continue. At one point she said, "I *won't* let him get me," with a look of such determination that one could feel only humility. If she can do this, then surely I can. This is an ordinary woman, in a conservative skirt and blouse. You would never recognize her on the street for a warrior.

I am furious with the person who violated this woman. I want every perpetrator of such abuse to have to look upon what he or she has done, the results of a lack of empathy. I want the perpetrator to feel the pain of the witness and to have the witness's knowledge that his or her own distress is nothing in comparison to what the recipient of the abuse endures.

I am grateful to the woman who permits me to stand next to her. In so doing, I learn something of human courage and something of myself.

ಜಿ 1996 ಡಿ

Ripped Open

A year and a half since I've written. My mother's unexpected death tore a hole in my life. I've been lost, occupied with my pain and with managing my life and not much else. Everything is changed. My experience in some fundamental way is now divided into "before" and "after."

It's difficult to pick up the threads of thinking about my work through this writing. Partly I feel rusty—an apt metaphor, if trite—like the water coming from an unused pipe, dark with sediment and disuse, spitting out in great unnerving bursts and then . . . nothing. I look anxiously at the faucet, doubtful that anything potable will ever emerge.

Partly I don't know how to cross the gulf between then and now. My world is changed and I'm changed because my mother has died. But in these two years, therapy is different also. With insurance changes, fewer people have the option of seeking therapy for more than quick symptom relief. I worry about how to position myself professionally in anticipation of market forces that I don't understand. I see more clients less often for less money. I wonder if, when all is said and done, the practice of psychotherapy will be recognizable. Even if it is, will it be something that I can bear to do, let alone love to do? Will it still have any heart? Will the satisfactions be worth the costs?

It is so difficult to be facing these questions just at the time that I'm also facing this deep personal loss. If my mother's death dropped me into the center of some heaving gray sea, I have swum to shore only to find quicksand where there should be reliable ground.

Managed Care Rears
Its Ugly Head

APRIL 16, 1996

It's been harder than I thought it would be to get started writing again. Some of that is just losing the habit, I think. I can have a chunk of time, use it up doing other things, and then realize with a sense of disappointment that it didn't occur to me to write. Some, perhaps, is part of how I stand in the world these days. I've experienced some major difficulties in the past few years. I am still struggling with how to live in the context of ongoing suffering. Some is a response to the way therapy and health care delivery has changed. Therapy is increasingly becoming a matter of techniques, of finding the most efficient solution to the problems that can be the most clearly defined. I find that the engagement of my heart is not called for as often as is the engagement of my skill. Skill is satisfying, yes, but not much to write home about.

I just spoke with a woman who works for a managed care company. I'm considering applying to join their panel of service providers. The contract, obviously written by a bevy of lawyers who work somewhere urban, is a nightmare of definitions and constraints. To their credit, they have removed the "gag clause" from an earlier version, the section that prohibited me from saying anything to anyone that might reflect negatively on the managed care company. Last I knew, even psychologists had First Amendment rights. But there's still a clause in the contract that says I must be available twenty-four hours a day, seven days a week within two hours of a call. How does one individual in private practice do that? And have anything approaching a normal life, I mean.

It seems increasingly clear that the only way to survive will be to band together in larger groups of providers (to be able to provide the kind of backup required), with more hours of clerical support (to respond to the reporting requirements). Better yet, I would be wise to do what so many of my colleagues are doing and look for part-time work in another setting. I imagine psychotherapy gradually (or maybe not so gradually) splitting into the large group practices that work with managed care, the therapy factories that will offer quick pre-formulated solutions to carefully circumscribed difficulties, and the outside-of-the-system renegades who don't need a reliable income to survive. There will always, of course, be other options available to the wealthy who can afford to contract independent of insurance and pay for privacy and for time. How many therapists will be left to do that work? There are only so many wealthy people to go around. Not enough in this area, anyway, to support more than one or two therapists. I can see what seems to be happening along these lines. The therapists who are able to avoid working with managed care are those who don't need to support themselves fully through their work. They are either partly retired or supplementing other income. Some are talented people with the good fortune or the age to be able to be semiretired. And some are "dabblers," people who are intrigued by therapy but who have limited training and limited experience.

What it all adds up to is a kind of deprofessionalizing of psychotherapy. If therapy is redefined as a quick fix, then any trained paraprofessional should be able to administer a step-by-step behavioral program. If the alternative definition is a kind of self-absorption indulged in by the well-to-do, who wouldn't look down one's nose at that?

Maybe it won't come to that. But I notice that when I think of therapy as powerful and humbling, the way it always used to seem to me, I feel as though I should be slightly embarrassed, like I'm saying something hopelessly out of date.

Life's Vicissitudes

APRIL 24, 1996

It's been snowing off and on all day today, the thermometer holding at a dispiriting thirty degrees. Not that we have any accumulation to show for it, which allows me to cling to some shred of hope. Outside I can see the crocuses and scilla holding their own. There's even a robin hopping in my perennial bed, apparently unconcerned. I know that in a couple of weeks spring will have blasted forth in the usual jet-propelled manner of the North Country. But today I am a bit droopy, my mood tied, predictably, to the whims of the weather.

Therapy often has weatherlike swings as well. Although I have a general sense of what's going on with people, my expectations are often proved wrong. Yesterday a man who had presented himself as simply in need of support in a difficult life period came in saying that he felt so unable to manage that he wondered whether he needed to be hospitalized. He had happened to run into his ex-wife on the way to his appointment with me, and the encounter had pressed home to him some deep longing and anger that he carries about the loss of that relationship. This man is physically ill but in fact has a reasonable network of resources. Yet those resources don't seem to be making any difference in how bereft and angry and helpless he feels. As he spoke, I gradually saw beneath the professional facade to the high-stakes and desperate meaning of his illness. He is gambling everything, perhaps even his life, on the hope he has had since childhood that if he is sick enough, if he needs them enough, then his alcoholic parents will finally have to really take care of him. Of course, in this case it's his ex-wife that he's focused that expectation on, and maybe it will come to be me as well. But at heart it's mom and dad. It's the old question: "Who will be there for me?"

My other surprise was from a woman who has a history of sexual abuse by her stepfather. For the past few months, she has labored to take that abuse seriously, to believe that it was as destructive as it felt, to trust that her pain is legitimate and deserves attention. Since I saw her last week, she got a call from her sister, telling her for the first time that she also was also abused by their stepfather and that she knew of three other girls from the Little League team their stepfather coached who were similarly targeted. Knowing that, something cracked open for my client. There was no longer any way that she could think she deserved the abuse, that it was some quirk of her character. With that phone call, her stepfather went in her mind from an abusive parent to a criminal, someone stalking and damaging any girls he could get access to. She kept saying, "It's not me; it's *him*." For the first time, she is seriously considering confronting him with the truth. When I first met her, she still felt obliged to visit her parents even though her stepfather continued to make sexually suggestive comments to her. The idea of doing so now would strike her as ridiculous. When she talks about her stepfather, what happened, and her choices now, her sense of personal power is obvious. If six months ago she was all tears, she is thunder now. I watch her with joy.

Funny how change works. As I've been writing this, the sun has finally emerged. It's late in the day for it to do much good. But still, it's there. My business is creating change. I put everything I can into knowing how to do that. I know that the man would have revealed that deeper layer to me sooner or later, and that the woman would have eventually come to see her stepfather for the predator he is. But sometimes the moment of change itself is like the weather, miraculous and recondite, as layered in life's vicissitudes as sudden sun after late April snow.

For Love and Money

I've had something of a cash flow crunch lately. It is a consequence of being hit particularly hard with taxes this year, combined with insurance companies' decisions to pay me less. I usually have the luxury of having enough money that I don't have to be concerned about what's going on with any individual client. I can be generous about allowing people to catch up with overdue bills gradually and unconcerned with whether a particular insurance check is slow in coming. But lately I've been looking eagerly for the mail to see if any insurance checks have arrived and noticing anxiously who is paying me on time and who is not. It's awkward that the caregiving of therapy is exchanged for money. Some people take it in stride, casually writing checks for each session, without any apparent feeling one way or the other. Others feel resentful (although they often would not admit it even if asked) that, essentially, they have to pay their mother. How outrageous! If I truly loved them, surely I would love them without recompense. And the truth is that there's something to that. My caring, after all, cannot be bought. But my skills and time can be. It is how I pay my bills and hope to fund my retirement.

What's hardest, I think, is to separate out the real constraints of people's financial resources from the choices they make about how to use the resources they have. I find sliding-fee scales based on income unfair. Income alone does not take other funds into account (e.g., inherited wealth) and is unresponsive to financial obligations. I have known people living on unemployment insurance to be reasonably comfortable paying me an amount that matches what a woman with a good job but three young children's day care to consider can manage. So I ask people to tell me honestly what they can afford, and we negotiate from there.

This, as you can imagine, opens me up to a stunning array of responses. Some people, particularly "old lefties" and political progressives, understand the "from each according to his ability" theory without trouble. They pay what they can, adjusting for circumstance. Often, these are the people who will report without fanfare, "I got a raise at work. I can pay you five dollars more now." Occasionally clients are really at sea, used to being told what they must pay (often along with being told everything else they are supposed to do) and keep asking me to tell them what they can afford. More often than I like to think, people choose something that feels reasonable to them, but later circumstances reveal a big difference between what they are comfortable paying and what they can really afford.

What am I to think of a client who pays a reduced fee, owes me money, and then takes a trip to Europe (although I know he or she has had to scrape together the money to do that)? Of someone who is paying a reduced fee but then wants to come more often (at the same fee)? If he or she can afford the greater frequency, doesn't that suggest that he or she could have afforded a higher fee when he or she came less often? What do I say to a man who is living off a trust fund, not employed, and wants a reduced fee because it is, in fact, what he can afford based on the amount he gets from the trust fund? How about the woman with a reasonably good job who chooses to pay off an overdue bill at the rate of five dollars a month?

Of course, on the other hand, some people truly cannot afford to pay full fee but can't live with the idea of not paying their own way. I have sometimes been in the odd (I am a business person, after all) position of talking someone into paying a lower fee. Those are easier, though, at least for me. I get to be generous in the context of looking at the person's difficulty with accepting help. The other extreme is harder. In the first place, people are rarely aware of the meaning of their choices about money, and often will protest vigorously when I suggest that more might be going on here than meets the eye. But, more important, I don't like feeling greedy. Or perhaps it's more a matter of not liking to appear greedy.

It's too tempting to collude with the client in creating an illusion that I'm really only doing this work for love and the money is a sort of half-ignored and unimportant by-product. Again, there's some truth to that. In fact, much of why I do this work is essentially for love. But I also want to make a good living. Money recompenses me for the enormous responsibility involved in committing to the healing of another human being. Once, when I was working at a politically progressive institution, someone suggested that all employees should be paid the same regardless of their job. *Fine,* I thought immediately, *I'll sweep floors.* The truth is that although therapy is deeply rewarding in many ways, if I were not paid at least moderately well for it, I would do something that cost me less personally. I fantasize sometimes about that kind of job: the job you don't take home, the one that doesn't ask that you use your heart and soul in the work. Of course, it is precisely because I must put my heart into my work that it is so satisfying. But it's emotionally expensive, too, and that expense is at least partly paid for with my fees.

Breath

Some years ago, at an intimate concert featuring a string quartet, I had the good fortune to be seated practically in the violinist's lap. Truly, I was close enough that I had to remember not to lean forward or his elbow would have poked me as he played. What struck me (no, it wasn't the elbow) was the elegant nonverbal communication among the musicians. As they began, there was a common intake of breath, cueing each of them for the precise moment to start.

We've had a late spring this year, and this moment in the season has that same quality: the breath before the sound, silent, or nearly so, but signaling inevitability.

Breathing is so richly communicative. The deep, shoulder-dropping sigh of release; the quick, constricted panting of anxiety, almost as if the air itself feels dangerous to the breather. In hypnosis, people usually breathe evenly. I speak with the rhythm of their breathing, a way of communicating accompaniment. In the deeper moments of therapy, when the person seems balanced on the knife edge of possibility, we very often breathe together, whether I intend it or not. It's a kind of empathy, I suppose, but I feel it as more than that. Is not the spirit connected to breath?

Transformation or Technician

JUNE 5, 1996

Sometimes it starts with just the tiniest of clues: the twinge of fear *here* but not elsewhere, the reaction that seems just a bit out of proportion. Often, what tips me off is my own sense that, in spite of how reasonable the person's explanation sounds, emotionally something just isn't adding up. It's a delicate moment, that—the quick intuition that the trouble lies behind this particular door and no other. And then the client's answering willingness to hold still for the probing, to follow in courage and curiosity the thread of the pain, to say more when instinct calls for evasion. Although one client did say to me recently, grinning and holding out her wrists together as if for handcuffs, "You'll get it out of me sooner or later. I might as well go willingly!"

It seems to me miraculous, no matter how often I take part. I imagine that midwives must feel the same. You know there's a baby in there, and yet when it appears, what can you feel but humility and astonishment? I've watched repeatedly as that subtle sense of something not quite fitting, when followed, enlarges and connects to the whole, shifting form and appearance several times until the moment when the client and I sit back relieved and appreciative and slightly surprised at the result. Well, who knew it was about *that?* Yes, I know what I do, could even tell you at each step, to make this possible. And a skilled client knows as well how to do the same, to talk about the thing that sticks out, that doesn't feel right, to say the feeling even if it's embarrassing or doesn't make sense. But understanding how to create something doesn't seem to preclude the feeling that the consequence sits somewhat apart from you, with its own life and reason for coming into being.

I once was dumped out of a canoe into deep rapids and almost immediately found my foot trapped under a boulder. In chest-high frigid water I worked to maneuver my foot out, pulling and twisting, getting panicky as I got increasingly hypothermic. Then, without warning, I was free. I struggled to the side of the river and the outstretched hand of someone who'd been fishing on the bank. I guess it makes sense that there are only so many ways to wiggle a foot and that eventually I must have found the perfect angle and pressure that would effect a release. But my response was bewildered relief, gratitude for a small wonder. Therapy is much like that: the subtle shifting and probing that seems aimless until something is abruptly freed up and the whole gestalt changes.

Therapy of this sort is the kind that transforms people. Of course, that includes the therapist as well. Its goal is to alleviate pain, but its result is not just the easing of a symptom but the restoration of the heart. It is not often quick, and not what insurance companies have in mind.

I spoke recently with a colleague who noticed that she didn't quite know how to talk with her clients without approaching them as whole human beings rather than conditions. But if therapists are to help with symptoms of depression or anxiety in six sessions, or even twelve, we cannot afford to do more than treat conditions. We will become like medical doctors, asking pointed questions about where it hurts and for how long, impatient with the person who veers off the subject to discuss her or his life outside the problem at hand. Perhaps that's as it should be. Although in some ways it's the medical equivalent of offering aspirin and a bandage to the young man in his fifth bar fight. With appropriate administration of aspirin and bandages, he can continue to fight all he wants, at least until the injuries are beyond aspirin. Is it or is it not the purview of health insurance to consider prevention and quality of life?

I wonder if I can make the transition. Can I become what I think of as a "psych tech," treating symptoms and conditions, hoping the person doesn't intrude too much on the treatment? Sometimes it feels fine. Sometimes someone truly only wants or needs help with the immediate distress, and it's a pleasure to be able to offer that. But it uses me poorly, like a poet being asked to write advertising jingles. There's a certain mild satisfaction when it's snappy and it rhymes, but it turns my vocation into a job—just a job.

It Takes All the Running You Can Do

I'm doing my usual "day off" routine, which consists of tearing through the day with an impractically long list of the things I'd like to get done, or must get done, or think I must get done. I'm not always sure which it is. I know that I feel relieved and satisfied when I get things accomplished, crossed off the list. But it's not as if I ever get to rest for any period of time and enjoy the results; there are always more things to add to the list. A friend refers to them as "ants." It's a good feeling when you get rid of an ant that is crawling around your house, and sometimes, briefly, there might even be no ants in sight. But there are billions of ants in the world, more ants than you can imagine, always more ants to replace the ones you sweep away. You could spend your whole life killing ants and it would have accomplished nothing.

So often I see clients who are in trouble at least partly because their lives are untenable when it comes to what they have to get done in a day. This is especially true of parents. Couples come for their therapy appointment, meeting breathlessly at my office. I hear them negotiating on their way up the stairs: "Can you pick up the boys at day care? I'll run to the store for groceries. Did you remember the dry cleaning? Who'll call the sitter for tonight?" They feel estranged from each other and any perceptive ten-year-old could tell them why: Their therapy appointment may be the only time they have for more than household management discussions. Time together? They're running from the start of the day until its close, sometimes staying up too late just to get a half hour to read or watch television. Who has time for a relationship?

I often feel as though I work all day during the week and then spend weekends at my "second job" of maintaining the house, the lawn, garden, laundry. It's not that I never have time to relax, but that time for relaxation seems constrained and stolen from all the obligations on The List. When I sit down, the house calls, "Clean me!" and the garden yells, "Weed me!" I wonder vaguely if retirement, still impossibly far away, will mean that I am not ruled by my commitments and the endless business of life. But I also feel anxious at the prospect. What if I got up and had nothing to do all day? It would be heaven for a few days, a couple of weeks, the length of a vacation. But after that?

The Overworked American describes the increasing workload of average people in the United States. The forces that drive this phenomenon are both economic and on the order of national character. But I think that we may also have come to depend on being overworked. We're addicted to the slight adrenaline rush, the feeling of "getting somewhere," or the illusion that being busy means being important. But, more centrally, being overscheduled is one solution to the fundamental existential dilemma. Who can think about why they're here and what their lives mean when faced with having to pick up the kids and get them fed in the next forty-five minutes, with the next dozen things on the list that must be done, with all those ants to be gotten rid of?

And Now, a Word from Mother Nature

I can see the first soft whisperings of autumn's color outside my window as I write this. I should go sit outside, really. It's so compelling to fill my time with all the duties that I seem to think are more important than simply being. Responsibility before pleasure. What a way to live.

Last Wednesday was Nature Sightings Day. There was a deer grazing under an apple tree as I walked in the morning. We stopped and watched each other. The deer wandered away after a while. It was not quite sure enough about me to stay but not worried enough to run. Later, digging in the garden, I went to get a shovel leaning against the house and startled a garter snake sunning itself, who in turn startled me. We repeated the exchange two or three more times as I traded the shovel for a pickax, brought the pickax back, got the shovel again. I apologized, but didn't see the snake on the last trip. I imagine it slid off in exasperation from having its nap interrupted too many times.

Late in the day I watched a hummingbird for a while; they won't be around much longer, I imagine. They're like thoughts: arrow quick and slightly unpredictable, almost seen from the corner of the eye and gone. I watched this one rest on a branch, perfectly disguised in plain sight because it is so tiny. Then a dragonfly caught my eye, patrolling back and forth repeatedly across the same small area. Supper patrol, I guessed. Every few sweeps it would pluck a minuscule insect out of thin air. Magic! Occasionally, I saw a dropped insect corpse. Or was it one that got away? Or the leftovers after the dragonfly had chomped off the yummy parts? Or just one that tasted bad, a reject?

Ah, I won't see these wonders sitting inside at my computer. And it's Sunday afternoon. The weekend is almost over. Responsibility can wait; I'm going outside.

Turning Gold into Lead

OCTOBER 8, 1996

How fast the season moves! Only a week and a half ago, perhaps, I looked out the window by my desk to see a single red maple trumpeting up from the surrounding green. Today, the color is already starting to go by, lingering with soft golds and faded oranges. A few days ago, early in the morning after a hard frost, I stood outside listening to the leaves fall. There was no breeze, just the icy snick, snick of each leaf detaching and hitting the ground. The leaves tonight rattle like seeds in a gourd. The woods are stripping down, just the essentials to meet the winter. I can't transition nearly so cleanly.

I made a mistake the other day. It was one I would not have made before the advent of managed care. A new client came in complaining of depression. Her insurance allows seven sessions. You can request more, to the tune of six forms, the time needed to fill them out, the uncertainty of approval, and the subtle worry that if I do this too often I won't be perceived as a "team player." A colleague in Oregon recently told me that one of her friends had been asked to leave a managed care panel because her average number of sessions was more than four. *Four.*

It seemed to me that this client could benefit from an antidepressant. I thought of our seven sessions, and I thought of how even with luck, an antidepressant can take a month to work. I urged her to see a psychiatrist and suggested she call me once she had done so. In the back of my mind was the hope of "saving" her few sessions for when I might be able to do more than hold her hand until the antidepressant worked. I told her as much. She left agreeing to make the appointment.

I talked with her yesterday. She had seen a psychiatrist and gotten a prescription. She was glad she had done so and said, "He really listened to me." She has another appointment with him next week. She suggested that she and I meet in three weeks.

Well, I got what I wanted, didn't I? But reading between the lines, it's clear that she did not feel that I had "really listened" to her. She did not find talking with me all that helpful. In my eagerness to be efficient, I lost the immediate needs of the person in front of me. People and their hurts are not efficient. We do not make transitions quickly. It doesn't seem to matter much whether I talk with people about their insurance limits. People think, "Seven sessions, great. Let's meet that long." How would they know how very limited that is? If you've never seen a therapist, seven sessions must sound like a lot.

Last weekend I was working outside and saw several flocks of geese overhead. You always hear them before you see them, gossiping with one another on the long trip south. It feels as though I can see the great rolling turn of the world toward winter in the curve of the geese against the sky. My profession seems to be turning toward winter as well. I hope that there will be a spring.

The Therapist Finally Matures

OCTOBER 30, 1996

The Feminist Therapy Institute conference was the weekend before last. As always, it was wonderful. It's such a relief to be with a group of colleagues where I feel met and understood in my work, where I don't have to explain. We ate ice cream together and discussed topics from aging to antiracism work to feminist child therapy. We toured New York's Chinatown in a downpour. I met a feminist therapist from Israel, and renewed an acquaintance with a colleague from England. I appreciated the many forms that feminist therapy can take: Jungian, object relations, body-centered work, behavioral. Although, in the ways that mattered most, we all spoke the same language.

One woman talked about closing her practice. She was tired of responsibility for others, she said. She had been doing that since she was eleven years old. Most of us, I imagine, have been responsible for others since childhood. She wanted her life to be focused differently.

She was not talking about burnout, as far as I could tell. She meant something far subtler. I had a long discussion with a friend later, looking for what that something else was. I've felt it myself, a kind of thinning of the enthusiasm I used to feel. It's not that I no longer love my work; I do. It's not that I'm overwhelmed or burned out; I'm not. It's a layered thing, I believe, no one element but a series of them.

Some, undoubtedly, is the change in the health care system that has meant more hassle and, sometimes, less satisfying work. I have two masters now. One is, as it always has been, the sense that the client and I have about what's best for him or her. But the other, insidious and hidden, is the insurance industry and its secret numbers. Do I take twelve sessions to help someone with panic attacks when my colleagues take nine? What if an antianxiety medication can do the job in two visits to a physician? Someone is keeping tabs. This becomes more and more a part of how I negotiate with the client about what we can accomplish.

But some of it is certainly a kind of move toward health on my part. I would guess that everyone drawn to practice psychotherapy has some deeply embedded need to help, to make a difference, to ease pain. As we should. But such motivations aren't just inborn, like eye color. They're learned. Learned, generally, in response to our helplessness in the face of the pain in our families, or our training in being in charge of our parents' emotional well-being, or any number of garden-variety neurotic arrangements. Don't get me wrong. I'm really not saying anything like the old myth that therapists are crazier than the rest of the population. I think that all real vocations are probably neurotically driven. In fact, making good use of one's neuroses in one's work is a fairly healthy solution to the quirks and anxieties we all carry. But it seems to me that, with time, the solution of being a therapist has actually worked. That is, I've had a lot of experiences in my job of getting to tell the truth and making a difference with people's pain and being responsible in a loving effective way. I've felt and shown acceptance in response to a range of human oddities and failures. In some deep way it's finally registered. And it feels as though neurotically speaking, the thrill is gone. I find many other ways that my work is satisfying. Chief among them is the gratification of doing something skillfully. But it's not compelling in quite the same way.

Another aspect seems to be simple maturation. There are two parts to this. One—I'm not sure about this, but I wonder—is that perhaps it takes more effort to connect well with a range of people. When you're young, say, in your twenties, it's easy to find friends. Partly, I think, this is because you're not very well defined at that age. Lots of people are interesting and seem at least partial matches. As I get older, I'm much, much more discriminating about my friendships. I know who I am and what I'm looking for. In the same way, I wonder if it takes more energy to make a connection with someone quite different from yourself when you're forty-five than when you're twenty-five. It seems as though that might be true.

Maturation seems to bring a kind of self-acceptance, accelerated, perhaps, by the practice I've had in accepting my clients. And any lingering reservations I may have had about letting people see or respond to my hurts were blown apart in grieving my mother's death. (It brings to mind a client who told me that being in labor with her first child pretty much took care of any notions of modesty she might have left. I imagine that it's nature's way of preparing parents for children in the clingy stage who won't let them go to the bathroom by themselves.) I feel much more transparent as a therapist. We are all up against something; we are all on the road together. I don't need to be ahead of someone to lend a hand.

Also related to maturation—and I feel absolutely sure about this one—is that because it's clearer to me that I have limited energy, emotionally as well as physically, I am fiercer about balance in my life. I am not interested in relationships where I don't get something back. In therapy, this means that I feel more cautious about how many people I will see at a reduced fee. I'm more aware of how much "extra" is being asked of me, and more conscious about what I feel able to give.

In a way, therapy feels more like a job to me. I think that's good. It's less of my identity, less of how I know I matter. Being a therapist is so seductive. If you do anything even approaching a reasonable job (perhaps even if you don't), you become very important to a number of people. It's nice to feel important, especially after years of being a downtrodden student. Looking at my early essays, I often see a theme of astonishment at feeling so important. I was (and am) too much of a feminist to be seduced. But I was taken with it. Now a client's experience of me as important feels as though it washes right by. It's only his or her feeling, a simple by-product of his or her need and appreciation for help in changing. I've felt it myself with caretakers. It has little to do with me. Further, belief in my importance too easily becomes a kind of perfectionism, a holding of myself to high standards because a misstep feels unconscionable in the face of the client's need. Now I hold myself to high standards because work well done is more rewarding and because people deserve the best I can offer. I have ceded a bit more responsibility to the client. Therapy is something I find satisfying and that I do well. Really, that seems like plenty. Doesn't it?

I've been wondering, off and on, if the ways I'm feeling differently about my work over the past few years is a bad thing, a sign I'm burning out or still too caught up in my mourning process to give whole-heartedly, or so distressed by managed care that I can't enjoy my work the way I used to. But I think now that although there may be elements of those things, the truth is far more complex and, perhaps, far more positive. If I'm less motivated neurotically, I can offer help that is less contaminated. If I'm zealous about balance in my work, my clients will intuit that what I give is what I want to give, without strings attached. If a certain passionate gleam in my eye has dimmed, it means that I need less from my clients and from my work. I don't feel anywhere close to closing my practice. But I listened with interest to my colleague's story in a way that I would not have done several years ago. Perhaps I've been closing my "neurotic practice" for years!

A Punch in the Gut

He decided to see a therapist because he wasn't sure whether he wanted to divorce his wife. They'd grown apart over the years, he said. What talking they did do was more and more often irritable rather than friendly. This is fifteen years of marriage; they have three children.

I routinely ask about the rest of people's lives, their lives outside of the problem. He said he had no friends to speak of, no friends he could open his heart to, that is. He thought he might be afraid of close friendships. His parents? Well, he'd been "given away" by his parents when he was two years old. No, he didn't know why. He went to a foster home, luckily a stable one. Except that his foster mother died when he was ten. He went to live at the home of a friend, a warm family who wanted to adopt him. But he had long ago learned his lesson about attachment, and he refused. Why set yourself up?

This man is deeply injured about attachment. He feels distant from his wife because he feels distant from everyone. The closer the relationship is, the more danger it poses to him. Without help, his future, at least psychologically, is grimly predictable. He will leave his wife, probably in fact, but at least in feeling. His children will thus learn the same hard lessons of loss that he learned when young. He will have an affair or remarry, and will repeat the pattern in the new relationship: hope followed by distance followed by loss. He will do adequately in his life, crippled but not destroyed, but he will never know love that endures. He will always be a bit sad, a lot lonely. He will pass his pain on to his children.

I can help him, but it will take a long, life-changing therapy—a therapy of relationship. He will not trust me for many months, maybe years. It will take the security of time and predictability. He needs, in effect, one more chance at having a parent, at a relationship with a caregiver that he can depend on, who doesn't leave him either through choice or necessity. But I can give him that. And given that, he can rejoin the world of relationship, can learn to risk loving again.

His insurance will cover seven sessions.

Still Hurting

DECEMBER 4, 1996

It has been over two years since my mother's death. I'm all right, mostly; there's a layer or two of skin over the wound. I don't think about it for hours at a stretch. Days can go by with only fleeting thoughts. I enjoy myself in my life. And I will date time for the rest of my life from that loss. The world feels less secure, less hopeful, in some kind of irrevocable way. I still weep far more easily than I used to. Tragedy of any sort has an immediacy that never used to be the case. My god, I think, when I see the faces in the newspaper photo, the next-of-kin to the plane crash victims, the family of the person murdered, their anguish ghoulishly displayed on the evening news, I know how they feel. I don't want to know this, but I do. Sudden and unexpected death may still be anonymous, but it will never again feel impersonal.

I wonder how much more ease I will get from additional time. In the meantime, though, a personal familiarity with trauma is disgustingly helpful in my work. This is not my idea of a reasonable job qualification. But then again, maybe I don't have a reasonable job.

ଈ 1997 ଔ

Trying to Stay Sane

JANUARY 15, 1997

I went to the movies Saturday and saw *The English Patient*. It was beautifully filmed, powerfully acted; I'm sure it will win lots of awards; and I hated it. I was depressed and cranky leaving the film. I kept muttering to my companion, "I just spent two and a half hours of my life putting *yet more* images of trauma and sorrow into my unconscious." My companion, of course, thought the film was great. Everyone I've talked to thought the film was a "must see." There should be a caveat that comes with these kinds of movies, a surgeon general's warning (where is our psychologist general?): "A must see except for therapists."

Some of it was a matter of timing. Most of Friday afternoon I accompanied people with particularly difficult PTSD (post-traumatic stress disorder), listened to their nightmares, their flashbacks, evil images of betrayal and torment. I went home satisfied with the work, but drained. I can accommodate trauma when seeing it has a purpose, as in therapy. Trauma in the movies just feels gratuitous to me. And I'm due, overdue, for a vacation. I have not yet mastered the art of timing my vacations properly, perhaps because the exigencies of life complicate the decision so inconveniently. By the time I realize that I need some time off, it would be best if I left immediately. Naturally, that's not how it works.

There's a whole art to keeping oneself emotionally healthy while doing the work of therapy. The daily aspect of this is most important, I think. Am I exercising regularly, getting enough rest? Is my caseload manageable, both in the total number of people I'm seeing and the proportion of people who (although often rewarding) are particularly emotionally expensive to me? Do I get support and consultation from my colleagues? Am I having enough fun? Enough downtime?

Do I take time to read, to see my friends, to go to movies that are nothing like *The English Patient*?

I'm supervising another therapist who ignored this kind of attention to his needs: the sin of grandiosity. Rescuers all, therapists as a class are vulnerable to it, I think. There's a lot of pain out there. The economic uncertainty of private practice is scary, and it's very tempting to accept that one more client, that additional phone call at home, to postpone the vacation, to let work gobble up your time until it stands bloated and triumphant at the center of your life. The therapist I'm supervising paid when something broke inside him and he used a client to meet his own needs, the needs he'd pushed aside because he imagined he was made of different stuff than the rest of us.

I now have a vacation scheduled in two and a half weeks. I scheduled a massage for later this week. And I have renewed my vow to see only comedies when I decide to take in a film.

God Visits the Therapist

Today there was a message on my answering machine from a woman who's been working with me for a few months on trauma-related flashbacks and nightmares. We've been using EMDR (eye movement desensitization reprocessing), a new technique for trauma, that seems like nothing so much as snake oil hocus-pocus. I am always a bit apologetic when I offer it to clients, as with something slightly indelicate, as if I had a mouse by its tail and were handing it to them, eyes averted. It seems too improbable to be true. *Look, I'll give you this mouse if you want, lots of people have found it amazingly helpful. But please don't assume I'm personally in favor of mice.* Of course, that's the complicating factor: the damned thing seems to *work*. When this client was referred to me, her therapist asked what percentage of the people I'd seen with flashbacks had been helped by EMDR. I thought, hesitated, and then with some embarrassment had to report that in all truthfulness, in my limited experience, it was, well, er, actually close to 100 percent. Hard to reconcile doing something that seems patently ridiculous with results such as that. Maybe it's only people's expectations at work here, the placebo effect of the promising new technique. Maybe in thirty years I'll feel like a fool for using it. But I will quite cheerfully make a fool of myself if I can get these outcomes with people.

Anyway, the phone call was to report a miracle. This woman has lived with a level of daily pain that most of us cannot imagine. Pain saturated her relational life, her sleep, her weekends. It seduced her to do cruel things to herself in an effort at control and relief. It distorted her habits of living, things that most of us take for granted, such as the ability to fall asleep, to breathe, to feel mostly okay unless something is wrong. She called to say that she woke the morning after our last session to find that the terrorists had left her internal home. That it was quiet inside. For the first time since she was a young child, she woke the way others do: she simply woke up.

EMDR is relatively quick, but it is not always easy. I watched as this woman looked out at me from the vaults of hell. I know now what it is to look into the eyes of a child who is being raped. I would call it courage, except that I know that such notions are the privilege of those who have been spared. She would call it desperate necessity.

I can't believe I do this for work. That I get paid to see the face of the divine. What's sacred if not the sun rising in the morning or one woman's emergence from crushing horror into the possibility of her own life?

There but for the Grace of God

I've been serving on an investigative committee, looking into the possible unethical conduct of a fellow psychologist. It's scary. This is not one of those clear-cut cases. The psychologist did not do anything egregious (e.g., have sex with a client). Most of it, in fact, was simply a matter of wrong judgment. Only, in this case, the wrong judgment resulted in someone's death.

From the notes, I can see that the psychologist thought this one through; it's not a matter of negligence. It's clear that there was a real effort to do what seemed best for the clients involved. It was not a matter of the psychologist's self-interest getting in the way. Oh, I can see places where the psychologist drew the wrong conclusion—that is, I can see them with the consequences spread out before me in the form of legal reports. I'm not so sure I would have seen them had I been in the same situation.

I know what it's like. Clients in your office say they feel like killing themselves. Or that they're "obsessed with" or enraged at someone else. Maybe they say it casually, as though they don't really mean it. Maybe they say it at the end of the hour, on a Friday when you're going away that weekend. It could be that they have always seemed pretty reasonable, have never sounded impulsive or desperate. It might be your sure knowledge that if you insist on outside involvement, on the police or a hospital, that you will lose forever any possibility of an alliance with them. Perhaps they even give you assurances that they didn't mean it, that they're okay now. But how can you be sure?

It's not as impossible as it sounds. At least in some ways it's not. There are ways to assess risk, safeguards short of hospitalization or calling the police. But looked at another way, it is at least as impossible as it sounds. "Assessing risk" is only a fancy term for making an educated guess, a judgment call. I have many times taken a leap of faith with a client who was seriously suicidal, desperate not to have to go to the hospital, and agreed to what I hoped were enough safeguards that I could trust the person was adequately protected. The key word here is trust. In each of those cases, I have had to trust the client, trust that he or she would indeed call me if he or she felt badly suicidal, for example. If the person did not, then I would be in the same position as my colleague, with others scrutinizing my judgment. Rightfully so, on the one hand, given the magnitude of the result. Yet, in the final analysis, it's only a judgment and can be justified only so far. With the strength of the outcome on the side of error, what therapist can say that he or she made the best possible judgment?

I suppose that this kind of responsibility is partly what therapists get paid for. Yet it's terrifying to recognize on just how flimsy a foundation that responsibility often rests. I will scrutinize my colleague's decisions carefully. But I will remember that much of what separates us is chance.

The Trauma Attack

MAY 11, 1997

She came to her appointment weeping already, immediately after a fight with her husband. Anyone is upset after a bad fight, but this woman was clearly in a trauma crisis. Her husband's harsh words had been completely unexpected. He had used a phrase that her father used to say—that he used to say at night, when she curled terrified in her bed, half pretending to be asleep, half scrambling to get away from him. Her bed was set next to the wall. She recalls trying to flatten herself against it, clawing the wall itself, as if this time she might escape. She had been seven years old. She had almost forgotten that phrase; her husband didn't know.

It is over forty years later, and she weeps with the gasping shudders of a seven-year-old who could not afford to cry when the daddy who said he loved her hurt her so far inside she still can't find all the pain. It is between her legs and inside her belly and planted like evil seeds in her spirit, ready to sprout with violent suddenness after a fight with another man who loves her. But this time she is not seven, and miraculously has gotten in her car and come to her meeting with the mother—me—who, this time, will listen and somehow help.

I feel both impossibly small and very large. I am only my flawed self, big-eyed at the courage her trust implies. I have no magic up my sleeve. The damage is done. But in such a moment, I also have all that is necessary: my presence, loving and fiercely protective. I have the priceless knowledge given me by other clients who entrusted their pain and hope to my care. And something else: a practiced ability to recognize the direction of health and to use that as it emerges in her, and as I feel the pull of it in myself.

She works to say what she feels. I tell her what I can of why this is happening so that she doesn't have to be so frightened. She pulls herself, with effort, back toward me, away from the tendency to feel as though she's out of her body. I remind her that she has the power to act, to get support—power she did not have when she was seven. Her eyes are locked on me; she is in a light trance state. She says, "Tell me the thing about power again." I repeat it, changing the words slightly, with more passion. She is exhausted with fighting the destruction her father started, weary of bearing up, of choosing not to die. I throw the weight of my being into the fray on her side. To the extent that I have any influence at all, he will have to get past me to get to her, and I tell her as much. Metaphorically, I have placed myself in a position of protection, protection that she lacked from the mother who couldn't save her from the abuse. Gradually, I feel the balance shift. She has won, this time. Each win, each day that she lives well, moves her farther from hell's epicenter. I don't know if she can see that yet, but I can. Maybe that can be a light for both of us.

Learning Where the Edges Are

JUNE 23, 1997

It's such a pleasure when someone who has done life-changing work comes near the end of that undertaking. I talked today with one such woman. Both of us admired how far she had come. To rewrite one's whole emotional map of how the world works—how remarkable!

We noticed especially what had changed for her in the area of what therapists call boundaries, which really means the ability to say yes and no in relationships. That sounds easy, but it's not. To say yes, you have to know what you want, separate from what the other person wants. To say no requires a feeling of security that makes it comfortable to risk disappointing the other. For this woman, being able to say yes and no also meant that she had to feel clearly that she was in charge of her life and well-being. It meant she no longer needed to bend herself frantically this way and that in an effort to get someone else to respond to her the "right" way.

It was daunting at first. I remember the elaborate plans we made about what she would do to comfort herself when facing the great anxious void. How in the world could she teeter on the edge like that and not clutch at her partner to rescue her? How could she possibly feel secure, feel loved and lovable, if someone else didn't give her that? As a transition, I encouraged her to hold onto me for security, and I remember the sound of terror and of being lost in her voice when she would call. Today she still gets scared occasionally but sees it quickly for what it is, relaxes, and chooses differently. After a while, I know, even that discomfort will only come when she is most stressed.

I was lucky when it came to boundaries. My parents modeled responsibility for oneself and combined that with a respect for their children's privacy and a reasonable level of responsiveness. It wasn't perfect, but it was enough to teach me that I could take control of my own happiness. If your life belongs to you, boundaries come easily and naturally, without a struggle. Why expect another to provide something that is not in his or her control anyway? And conversely, why should I expect myself to give something that is not mine to give? The first of those has helped me in relationships, I think. The second has made it possible for me to be a therapist.

My clients hope for much from me: that I should be the mother they never had, that I might make them happy, that I could save them from the pain of life in general or of their particular lives. I can do none of those things, no matter how powerful their longing or how legitimate their need. But if I can stay relaxed in knowing those limits, where my power ends and theirs begins, I communicate implicit confidence in their ability to see to their own well-being. And, more important, I am free to offer the one thing that we can offer to another soul in pain: company.

The Knowledge of Death

I noticed texture and form when I was out walking this morning. The tamarack branches filigreed against a powdery sky, three or four kinds of ferns layered and dense along the side of the road, the scalloping of the maples, the elderberry umbels like a plate of beads. I'm stunned, blown away, when I pay any attention to it. Mostly I don't even look, caught as I am in my foolish thoughts.

Today I have to go to a friend's funeral. Watching her decline from cancer the past couple of months has been a lesson in attention to life's mundane pleasures. Three or four weeks ago she became unable to keep down solid food any longer, and mentioned wistfully that she would not be able to eat again. Not eat again! Ever, for the rest of your life! Her partner mentioned that a few days before she died someone was sipping a nonalcoholic beer and she asked for a taste, just to taste something again. Just to taste something. I taste things every day, often gulping my food because I'm in a hurry or reading the paper and not noticing. *Yep, this is good,* I'll say casually, assuming that I can have something else good later, and tomorrow, and forever.

One of my clients lost her mother recently and is in that first raw rush of grief. Sitting with her, I sometimes feel old, although she is the elder between us. I remember seeing my mother suddenly look older when her mother died; loss ages us, the aging effects of knowledge and of pain. Sometimes I have to work in the session to quiet myself, my own grief scraped open in my empathic response to my client. *Breathe,* I remind myself. *Her pain, yours is separate.* I wait to respond until I know I won't cry. Most of the time in therapy, my experience of what is helpful and appropriate to say is so deeply embedded that it feels as though I can say whatever comes to mind. In this situation, I weigh carefully, knowing that my impulse is to say too much, to leak my own experience of grief into the therapy. Like a novice, I scan every comment to be sure it is helpful to her and not a response to my own need. *You can cry later,* I remind myself. Sometimes I do.

If we play it right, the knowledge of death can sharpen our appreciation of life. I get pulled both ways, between depression and transcendence. I want transcendence—who doesn't?—but wanting doesn't make it so. I don't know what makes it so—maybe practicing enjoyment? Maybe watching the sky when I walk, delighting in my food. I'll let you know.

Heroes

I dreamt that I was on some kind of heroic quest (unidentified) and, at the moment of the dream, was in trouble and needed to get away from danger. I ran with my companion to a house, thinking I might be able to crawl under the porch. The woman who lived there invited us in and gave us something to eat. In the dream I knew, the way that one does in dreams, that there were two levels of reality: the mythic and the everyday. I knew that most people lived in the everyday reality and could not see the mythic one that I inhabited on my quest. In my dream, the woman who took me in could see that mythic reality, as if out of the corner of her eye, and acted on the basis of that vision. I was immensely grateful. It made all the difference that someone saw the truth of my situation and could simply help. It meant that I could relax from having to hide and scrounge and worry.

I think of my clients as heroic, too, some on occasion, some more consistently. She yanks her life back from the monster who would eat her alive, the demon who went after her body when she was a child and now wants her soul as well. He stares down the dragon, the one that whispers that he's worthless, that seduces him with despair. These people don't want to go out there and be brave. They sit in my office and change the subject and look for another way out and wish I would do it for them. But in the end, most value their freedom more than their fear. As others have noted, courage is not a matter of being fearless. It is a matter of acting anyway.

I am the one who must look out of the corner of her eye and see the mythic quest behind the facade of the tired lawyer or the harassed single parent sitting in the chair across from me. I want to offer one place where people don't have to pretend that they feel just like everybody else, that it's business as usual for them. One place where they can tell the truth, strategize, and maybe even get a snack for the arduous battle ahead.

Sucking the Soul out of Therapy

OCTOBER 3, 1997

I just finished a heart-wrenching conversation with a colleague. She's got the same thing I've got, only worse. The same thing so many of us have. She's anxious, not sleeping. Maybe a bit depressed, too. She feels the worst when trying to resume work after a vacation—not just the usual pangs to see the vacation over, but real pain at the notion of returning to her office. And I can see her point. She feels that her work has slowly, over the past few years, been drained of its meaning and satisfaction. It feels more like a job and less like a passion. She's not sure how much good she's doing, how much of a difference she makes. She's wondering about trying to find something else to do for work.

She's talking about managed care.

I'm a terrible consultant. I have little of use to tell her. Maybe we can figure out how to shift the balance a bit with a combination of things. Being a therapist has always been one of those gifts: a meaning-dense job. Maybe she can lower her expectations, not hope for so much of a feeling of making a difference. After all, lots of other jobs don't offer a feeling of purpose. Maybe she can cut back on the passion with which she approaches her work and use some of that spark to follow other interests, find other sources of meaning. I thought of myself and of the writing and editing I've been doing lately. I hadn't looked at it in this light before, but the timing of putting more energy into that coincided beautifully with the expansion of managed care, now that I think of it.

At the least, she can make sure she involves her clients in responding to the insurance limits. She can do the paperwork with the client, explain the limits of the insurance and make sure the client understands how these affect therapy, join with the client in choosing a response to that. This is my approach, partly because I feel it's more respectful (I'd certainly want to be in on decisions made about me; I'd want to know what paperwork was in my record), partly so I don't get resentful from shouldering the (unpaid) time and effort required all by myself, but largely so I'm not in some terrible conflict of interests. The pressure from the insurance companies is to provide less service; the client often wants more. If I don't make the conflict explicit, I will be in the position of trying to influence the client to use less service, really working on behalf of the insurance company, not for the client. The trouble is, even explaining the situation to clients and eliciting their involvement works only partway. Clients may still lobby for as much as they can "get," but I still know that if I support too many people with that approach, I will find myself on the outside of that insurance network. Oh, I know that there is a move for increasing piles of legislation to protect consumers from abuses in the insurance systems, but what this seems to translate to is simply more subtlety on the part of insurers. They will say, for example, that there are no limits on the number of sessions, and this is even true in a literal sense. The limits are still there, of course, just enforced differently: through increased paperwork, increased disfavor, increased aggravation. The clinician ends up feeling the way she or he is meant to feel: Why not make it easy on everyone and just keep the therapy short? Cost containment by harassment.

One insurer now wants to do the case review on the phone. The company will authorize only four sessions at a time, and it takes at least a month to schedule a phone appointment. Hmmm. With the phone review, I can still include the client if I use speakerphone. I called the company to check about this and it was clear that it would prefer that I not include the client "so that we can be more frank." I don't have anything to say that I wouldn't want to say in front of the client, so who has a problem with frankness? And why?

Whether we want it to or not, our approach is being shaped, at least somewhat, by what will be paid for. Most people cannot afford to pay for therapy on their own, at least not for any length of time. If someone comes in with an immediate problem complicated by a long-standing difficulty, let's say a problem in his current relationship complicated by trouble getting close to anyone, trouble making any relationship work, and his insurance allows for ten sessions, what should I work on with the person? Even if he theoretically has all the sessions he "needs," given that we must fill out plenty of forms asking for details about symptoms and goals and progress every several sessions in order to get these sessions paid for, do you think we will elect to do something about the life pattern? Unlikely. We'll sort through his current worry, patch the person up, and send him out to do it again. My colleague is right. How can this feel like making a real difference in someone's life?

Maybe, as the insurance companies argue, life change was never their business anyway. This is Western medicine, where we fix it if it's clearly broken, but we don't ask why it got broken in the first place, why it keeps getting broken, or how we can prevent further breaks. And maybe they're right. Maybe we, as a society, can't afford the luxury of helping people heal from the inside out. Maybe that should be the province of religion, or luck, or self-help. Mostly luck.

This colleague is a sensitive and talented therapist. I think the changes in the industry will shape us. Those who can't stand it will leave. And who will be left? Those comfortable with being more a businessperson than a healer. Those who enjoy quick in and quick out, those less comfortable with the intimacy and power and struggle of effecting lifelong change. Those who can live with feeling less effective, with losing opportunities to really make a difference. Those who have another source of income. Those who can do therapy as just another job.

I don't know where I stand with all this. I'm still sleeping nights. I've compromised and compromised, and I am still hanging in there. I count years to retirement over and over in my mind: *Let's see, if I work like this another dozen years, will I be close enough to retirement to be able to afford the loss of income if I just stopped taking managed care?* I try to reassure myself that I'm at least doing some good, that a little help over a crisis is better than no help at all. I get some feeling of meaning elsewhere. I pray (without much hope) that the system will loosen its greedy iron grip just a bit, enough that I can breathe. I wonder if I can somehow save more money and afford to make a lot less in ten years, in eight. I go to the office and do the best I can.

Ode to November

NOVEMBER 2, 1997

November. It's only humans' propensity for categorization that puts this month in the same season as the one before. November belongs to itself, as different from October as April is from May.

The leaves are mostly on the ground, just a few continuing to shimmer on the poplars. The locals call them "popples," which better captures their jauntiness. But most of what's left for foliage color is the tamaracks, like great gold feathers in the forest. The trees are beautiful, stripped down to their essential selves. Along the road, the old stone wall is also once again distinct. The color of the tree trunks matches the stone so closely that one can see they are cousins.

Surprisingly, what strikes me most about the season is its color. Impossible to describe, "brown" is completely inadequate for that softening of leaves on the ground, brown mated with red and gold and sand. Stripped of concealing leaves, the wild apples hang as conspicuously as in a child's drawing, inviting deer. This morning I saw a small green apple wedged in the fork of a maple tree, the work of a squirrel with a subtle sense of humor. Later in the month, November is sometimes no more than variations on the theme of gray, but now all is gold and rich brown and slate with the smallest of green accents.

No Winners Here

Last week I made what I have come to think of as "a managed care mistake," rushing in too fast to offer suggestions for changing the problem. "I need time to think," complained the client (who, thank heavens, was at least telling me why things felt off to her). "I don't want you to solve it for me." She was right, of course, and I confessed that I was feeling driven by the time-limited demands of her insurance. This is the kind of error that I would never (okay, rarely) have made several years ago. But this is now, and I no longer feel as though I have the luxury of allowing a solution to emerge from the client in its own time. If I can see a way through, I feel obliged to drag us there. I feel the way I imagine assembly line workers must feel when the line moves faster. Hurry, hurry, hurry! No time to chat with your neighbor. Watch your back or you'll be the next to go in this wave of industrial downsizing.

I hear my own clinical mistake echoed by a colleague who sees me for consultation. Although this is a skilled and experienced practitioner, when she consults about her work, I hear more and more often that she misses what once would have been obvious.

"Don't worry about it," this client reassured me. "We'll just get as far as we can in the time we have." But it's not that easy, I know. I can predict the outcome. We will make some, but limited, progress in the time allotted, and then she will want to ask the insurance company for more. She has made it clear that she cannot afford to pay for therapy herself. "Can't we work around the system?" she asks. Well, yes, but how do I begin to explain that this is not as straightforward as it looks? That there are other carrots and sticks built into the system, things that are generally unacknowledged, such as withholding part of my fee unless I keep my session numbers across clients below a certain level. This is similar to the way that one gets viewed as a "cooperative" or "difficult" clinician based upon how consistently he or she plays within the rules, and cooperative clinicians can get what they need when they really need it. This client expects to have therapy the way therapy used to be available: for a year or two without any need to focus on specific outcomes. I am already dreading having to try to explain to her insurer, in behavioral terms if you please, why such therapy would be "medically necessary."

Now, it is certainly possible that it would be helpful for this client to think more concretely about what she needs to change in her life, even if that approach is not her inclination. But it is just as possible that—gasp!—she knows what she needs. Unfortunately, what she needs is not what is available, not anymore. And while it's true that one can do a certain amount of finagling in approaching the insurance company, there are both limits to what one can reasonably expect to get away with and ways that one gets punished for pushing too hard.

The real problem here is that the interests of the insurers and those of the clients are at odds. Insurers claim otherwise, saying that they simply want greater efficiency, that they of course will authorize "necessary treatment." But I had one managed care company tell me that "necessary treatment" was "acute stabilization only." If a person is not in crisis, he or she doesn't need therapy. The bottom line is that the greatest interest of the insurers is the bottom line. The interest of the consumer is getting service. The two are compatible to a much smaller degree than everyone pretends. And because most insurers don't set absolute limits, the therapist is in the position of acting as an agent for the insurer, trying to get enough done as quickly as possible, if she or he values the continued ability to offer service at all. If she or he chooses to act as an agent for the client, trying to get as much as is best for the client, as much as the client feels necessary, the therapist will have to find some other means of economic support.

Clients, of course, can't be expected to be fully aware of all of this. The clients are focused on what they feel is best for them. I wish I could focus only upon what is best for them as well. It will look to these clients as if their therapists are unwilling to help them get what they want. It will look to me as if I am once again caught in the middle. I will feel messed over by insurance constraints and the clients will feel messed over by me.

৵ *1998* ৶

Panic

I just found out I had a "category 4" mammogram, the category before the one where they're sure it's cancer, the category where they want a biopsy. I feel sick, gutsick. I want to crawl into a hole and curl up and not come out. How the hell am I going to see clients? Although maybe seeing clients will be a relief, a respite to focus on someone else's life for a while. The challenge will be to muster the extra that everyone needs sometimes, the extra it takes to hold my ground when someone is caught and testing me, the extra needed when someone is in particular pain, the extra required to push someone who needs help getting to what's important. I don't have much extra. I need it all for myself.

Keeping Perspective

Seeing clients (after the bad mammogram and ensuing uncertainty) has generally been fine, in spite of my anxieties about doing so. I should have known; after all, I've been able to work even when reeling from the death of my mother, even while ill or otherwise distracted with personal distress. I guess I've never had such a scary threat to my own health that I needed to keep to one side while seeing clients. Who knows, maybe it will feel less possible to manage that if things get substantially worse. But for now I'm doing what I know to do: put it aside, focus harder on the other person. It takes an effort of will, but it works.

And, naturally, my clients help by continuing to enlighten and impress me! I was talking with a woman who has a history of repeated beatings and physical torture by an older brother—an experience guaranteed to teach you beyond a doubt that the world is devastatingly dangerous in ways that are hard to predict and impossible to control. She's trying to figure out how to feel safer. She told me that she's found something that works. When a challenging situation comes up, she asks herself, "Is my brother torturing me?" The answer, of course, is no. And, hey, if that's the case, whatever it is will be a piece of cake. I was delighted and stunned by the simple directness of her solution. It's true: if you've lived through the worst, you know everything else is easier. Don't sweat the small stuff—and it's all small stuff. Words to live by. A lesson for the therapist, she of the health anxieties.

Grounded

I've noticed a lack of inspiration in my work today. I did fine, but it was a pedestrian sort of fine, acceptable, workmanlike. No singing leaps of intuition. Although I haven't been thinking very much about it, today was the day I expected to hear from the breast care center about the next step they recommend. On some level that worry must have been there, like static, interference. Not enough to make working an effort, but enough to slow things down.

How much I take that intuitive ability for granted! I assume that I can hold openly whatever elements the client gives me and that flashes of insight, of possibility, will simply arrive. That I will know what's missing, what is secretly linked, or what needs to happen next. Today I listened to what my clients had to say and had—ideas. Not much to go on. One of my clients was using imagery as a medium and I usually speak imagery fluently. She would describe a imagined scene to me and I would think, "Huh." I'd try what was logical in a general way, and some of it was even reasonably accurate. But it sure as hell lacked fire.

I'm a magician; it's what I do for a living. Magic requires intention, but also something more, some ability to erase the self and reach for "an unfathomable Somewhat, which is *Not we*" (Thomas Carlyle). That's what I couldn't find today. Today I had to rely on my skill alone, the tool of professionals, not magicians.

The Therapist Lets Go

MARCH 10, 1998

A person has to be willing to fail in this business. I have a new client, a young woman in college. She has a remarkable mind. She is pursuing a career in science, and in high school walked away with some fancy science award. I'm captivated. *Oh, how wonderful,* I think, *the world needs more women in science.* She's going to a "name-brand" college now, and, as the song says, "[her] future's so bright, [she's] got to wear shades." Except that her drinking has been accelerating. Except that she parties instead of studying. Except that she's failing in school as she is in life.

She was in a car accident recently. She was driving drunk and was lucky to walk away alive. It scared her, and she says she "won't do that again," although what she means by that is she won't drive drunk. She doesn't plan to stop drinking. She doesn't see *that* as a problem. She was almost asked to leave the school last semester because her grades were so low. She can talk about what she wants for her future, but seems to have no intimation that the way she's living now just might jeopardize that future. If she flunks out of school, well, something will work out. It always has.

Her history, naturally, is what you might expect: abuse, early loss. None of this "bothers" her, though. She's happy to come talk to me. She seems to enjoy it, in fact. Her grandparents, her guardians, pay for the therapy. But she has no particular goals for the work with me. In fact, I would wager that she sees therapy as having mostly a comfort function: it's good to talk with someone; it feels better not to be so isolated. But that doesn't really have to do with her life.

I find myself feeling parental, in a way that's not very helpful here. I want to say all the things that I am sure her grandparents say, who, as she points out, "worry too much" about her. I worry too much, too. I want to shout clichés at her. You're throwing your life away! Don't you even *care;* you could have been *killed* in that accident! How exactly do you think you will realize those dreams of yours if you don't work toward them? Do you think someone's going to just hand you what you want? Where do you expect this way you're living to lead?

Of course, the truth is that although she has dreams for herself, she doesn't really expect to achieve them. She's not sure she even expects to live that long. She's a funny mixture of nonchalant acceptance of and pride in her gifts, and a recognition (at least when I point to it) that she doesn't seem to treat herself like she's worth much. She won't be able to take her therapy seriously if she can't take herself seriously.

The problem here, looked at from one angle, is that she's not in much of what she would call pain. Her hurt is visible to anyone who knows her, but not to her. Most people hurting that much would feel so awful that they would want to fix it, whatever it took. But her pain doesn't force her to do what she needs to, and her life doesn't feel valuable enough to her for her to do what she must in the absence of pain as a motivator.

If I allow her to drift through therapy, I collude with her not to take her life seriously. If I scold her, I take my place alongside all of the other well-meaning but ineffectual adults who want her to shape up, be different. Although I can hardly bear it, I have to be able to let her go, to let her destroy her future, if necessary. I will tell her I see that her pain is displayed to others but not to her. And I will say that she is the author of her life. I will offer possibilities and say that she must choose goals for herself in her work with me. Without goals, we have little reason to meet, at least now. Then I will let her go. It's my only hope.

Working While Drowning

MARCH 18, 1998

It has been a couple of weeks since Town Meeting. Winter lingers gently; it's been an easy one in spite of the usual dire autumn predictions based on the woolly bear caterpillar and other impeccable sources. At Town Meeting, we argued about the budget and reluctantly agreed to a compromise that would end a long-running feud with a neighboring town about whether we owed them money for ambulance service long since delivered and forgotten. We gossiped and joked standing in line through several paper ballots on hot issues, called for by those who suspected we might be better able to vote our consciences without the appraising looks of our neighbors if a show of hands were required. It only takes seven citizens to agree to a paper ballot for it to become fact. We lunched at long folding tables; for $3.50 you could choose among a dazzling array of variations on the theme of noodles, baked beans, jello molds, and unidentifiable casseroles, with pie and coffee for dessert. I love democracy: it tastes like pie and indigestion.

Town Meeting seems like a lifetime ago. Since then, I have had the special additional mammogram, and learned that I will indeed need a biopsy for the area that still looks suspicious. The biopsy procedure itself sounds dehumanizing and uncomfortable. This is my first real surgery, unless you count having my tonsils out at age five. The anxiety comes in waves, and sometimes I feel fine except for that small quaver in the back of my awareness. Sometimes.

The first couple of days after getting the news I would find myself occasionally losing track of things in sessions. Once or twice I got a tiny flash of irritation. *How can this person be complaining about something so small when I'm facing possible breast cancer?* I went so far as to think about whom I might seek out for supervision if I found these feelings intruding too much, aware that it's not just this breast cancer scare, but this as one in a series of life adversities that I've faced in the past few years. I can't be going unscathed. I have a colleague whom I consult with regularly, but I could imagine my need going beyond the limits of my informal peer consultation. Since then, I've settled down and rallied my friends. I seem to be holding my own at work. I'll keep an eye on it.

I've also noticed occasional feelings of "otherness" as I go through my day, looking at people on the street and thinking that they are fine, going about their business, healthy, that they inhabit some world I used to know but don't live in now. I remember feeling that way constantly when grieving acutely. Then the sensation was even stronger, feeling as though I couldn't even imagine what normal might be like, what it would be like to have nothing more on your mind and heart than what to make for supper or some minor conflict at work or something you had planned for the weekend. Except, of course, not everyone on the street is healthy or happy, regardless of how they look. I imagine I look "normal," too.

I remember walking for hours after work one evening over three years ago now, when my grief was fresh, too distressed to consider going home, looking at houses and lighted windows and wondering which homes had been touched by death, as I was. In pain, I imagine myself isolated. But perhaps suffering is more the norm, each of us with our own life drama, pain remembered or pain in the present, it hardly matters. I should know better. I know the inner lives of my clients, all of whom look fine, go to work, and live their lives, with what they're up against visible only to me and a few close friends or family. When I was newly grieving, I remember looking at myself in the mirror and being astonished that it didn't show except for a certain haggard quality. I still had eyes and a nose and a mouth, all in their usual places. Remarkable. As I do now; as do my fellow sufferers in my office or on the street. Perhaps Town Meeting wasn't as long ago and far away as I imagine.

Powerlessness and Joy

APRIL 5, 1998

The biopsy is over; the results are negative. How much summed up in that sentence! My life returned to me.

I am reading Polly Young-Eisendrath's *The Gifts of Suffering*. She would dispute this, would say that my life has not been returned to me because it never was separate from and disrupted by this cancer scare. Distress does not interrupt life, as if life were what happens when we are not in pain. Distress is life: the Buddhist *life is suffering*.

My life seems to have been a series of distresses over the past few years. I have indeed been conceptualizing them as interruptions in a way. "A rough spell," I've been telling my friends, and, "Do you think this is the last of them?" as each new one appears on the horizon. My friends, wiser than I, avoid the question. It's not really that I expect calm waters for the entire of my life, but more a matter of noticing a kind of condensed quality to all of this turmoil. When will it ease up, I wonder. How am I supposed to make sense of this?

I mostly feel as though I'm simply enduring it all, trudging along. Young-Eisendrath talks about transformation, but I only feel a kind of perseverance. And perseverance isn't even a particular virtue. What's the alternative? Yet when she describes what that transformation is composed of, I recognize bits of it in my experience. Increased compassion. Submission to dependence. Yielding to powerlessness. An ability to take the offering of the moment.

It's ironic because I've been staring right at it all the time. As difficulty after difficulty piled up in my life, I looked for meaning. But all I could figure out was that everything seemed to be telling me *Give up; you're powerless here. That can't be right,* I thought. If there's meaning to be had in all this pain, it must be something else. But there's powerlessness and then there's powerlessness. It's not the same. When I reflect on it, I haven't been feeling or acting as though there's nothing I can or should do. With this biopsy, for example, I rallied my friends and family, depended on my partner for distraction and support, blurted out how I was feeling to all who would listen, asked for "good vibes" to be sent my way during the procedure. I called the doctor and said I wanted Ativan (an antianxiety drug) to help me through the event itself. When I got the good news, I spent hours calling and e-mailing all the people who, I knew, were holding me in their hearts and thoughts. My powerlessness was not about my response, but about the pain itself, the fact of illness and anxiety.

And yes, I do need to learn something about that kind of powerlessness. I'm the organized sort, and I put a lot of energy into keeping my life in order. I plan for the future. I have life insurance, disability insurance, and insurance for my car and my home and against malpractice claims. And I should have all these insurances, just as I should have rallied my friends and family when I needed them. But no planning, no insurance, no amount of order can insure against the inevitable assault of pain in one's life, against the fact of my powerlessness over that. Living well, eating right, being good, taking care of business—all these things are worth doing for a variety of reasons, but not because they protect you. There is no protection.

I think I used to live holding my breath, in a way. Maybe if I did everything right, then I would somehow make it to my death without any major disasters. It's a seductive idea, the illusion of control, and not only because there's a smidgen of truth to it. But I can no longer continue to believe it. My health has been challenged, my beloved profession is under attack, someone I love is dead. What am I to make of this? Not that I may as well cancel my insurance policies or stop exercising. But perhaps that I may as well breathe easy.

Last weekend I visited my brother. I arrived at suppertime. My family was in the backyard, sitting on the deck with pizza and a bottle of wine. It was unusually warm and the air was soft and some tiny early daffodils were blooming. The biopsy was over and the results were negative. I got out of my car and walked toward everyone, and my niece and two nephews yelled my name in delight as they spotted me, running to me for hugs and kisses. I picked a couple of them up (too bad about the incision and "no heavy lifting") and thought, *Life is sweet.*

Grace

Yesterday morning was suffused with mist, retreating before me as I walked, like memories. Today all is bright-edged under the hand of spring. Our hearts go out to the rest of the country assaulted with impossible weather, but in New England, El Niño is the prince of weather systems, bringing us spring a good two or three weeks early after a mild winter. I read in last night's paper that the ice is out on Moosehead Lake in the Northeast Kingdom, something that generally happens in mid-May. (This sounds like a cartoon: "Vermont's idea of news.") It's such a joy to have the songbirds back, and I find myself half-consciously blessing them as I walk by: *May you find a mate*. But perhaps what I really mean is that they are so lovely that I would mate with them myself if it weren't an impossible interspecies proposition. Our offspring would have wings in spite of their earthbound mother.

One of the great pleasures of psychotherapy is watching your clients leave. A poignant pleasure, it's true, since I inevitably have come to love the person in some way, and I know that our relationship is not really mutual. I will not see them later at Thanksgiving dinner or catch up with them at a family reunion. And a client who leaves no longer needs me, and I may miss feeling so central to her or him. But, oh, the gladness I feel in watching someone fly! Anna Salter has an exquisite description of sitting with a client near the end of that client's therapy, thinking, "She has no idea how she shines." It's that. The hard winter in which we wept and bled followed by spring's softening. The emerging outline of someone no longer defined by pain. The loved other who wobbles out of the nest, makes a few trial flights with growing grace, and then soars.

The Noose Tightens

MAY 6, 1998

Today I got my first obvious kick in the butt from managed "care." It's about a client I've been seeing for several months now. That's a long time in managed care land, but not very long when it comes to the kinds of ways this client is trying to change: a lifelong pattern, well entrenched, that pervades every part of her life. She has been in therapy before without really getting to the root of the difficulty. Now, past midlife, she feels the motivation that comes with knowing you're not immortal. Will she really make herself the life she wants? I think she can, but I also know that she won't do it in several months.

We have used a diagnosis of depression, probably the best fit, and certainly one of the ways her pain shows itself. The phone message from the managed care representative said that in response to our request for fifteen more sessions, the company would give us three. I was to use the three sessions to refer her to a psychiatrist for anti-depressant medication. Since she still had symptoms after several months, the reasoning went, apparently therapy wasn't working and drugs were called for.

Well, I know I haven't been playing the game properly in this situation. This is not a client who can benefit from a quick set of tools or a bit of encouragement, not someone who was essentially fine except for a symptom or two. This woman is also not biochemically depressed. She will feel better when she makes fundamental changes in how she lives. Managed care is not interested in paying for fundamental changes.

I did recently have another situation that was somewhat similar, now that I think of it, although less distressing because I caught it sooner. As with this one, it involved a woman who was talking about lifelong difficulty in relationships. Unlike the first client, this woman didn't really have much in the way of typical symptoms: she wasn't especially depressed or anxious, she managed fine at work. She simply had never had a loving relationship with a partner and knew she always chose people who hurt her. She had virtually no friends. Alerted, I called the managed care company in charge of allotting her insurance money and explained the situation. We don't pay for "problems in living," the representative said. The client has a choice between paying for therapy herself or living the rest of her life at half-mast, the emotional equivalent of chronic arthritis. Hey, you can still hold a job with arthritis! Why treat it?

I have offered her the option of a reduced fee. We may choose to meet less often, perhaps every month or six weeks, and I can try to coach her through the work she needs to do. Maybe it will even work; I will be interested to see whether it does. I have my doubts, though. Her damage is in the area of relationship. The best way of changing that kind of long-term relational fear and insecurity is through the "corrective emotional experience" of a relationship with the therapist. It seems unlikely that she and I will develop much of a close relationship at the rate of an hour every several weeks. In fact, that kind of pattern repeats exactly what she has done her whole life: staying distant, hiding her true self, not getting what she needs. Managed care as repeat of the family damage.

I don't know what will happen with the woman whose request for more sessions just got turned into a demand that she take drugs. I'm fairly sure she does not see medication as a solution. As it is, the insurance company will only pay for half the cost of her sessions, after a hefty deductible. So I am already discounting her fee by a substantial amount. And, ironically enough, she has received no reimbursement at all for the sessions we've billed for, what with one snafu after another. Perhaps she will eventually get some of that money back, perhaps not. In the meantime, of course, the insurance company collects the interest on whatever payment it can find reason to delay. Maybe she will continue paying me out of her pocket, although I know it stretches her budget. If so, I will be relieved not to have to think about managed care, to be able to guide our work thinking only about what seems best for her. Of course, the insurance company will also be glad for that. To the company, that will be a success. Not a therapeutic success, but a financial success. Isn't that the bottom line?

The Terror Time

AUGUST 16, 1998

There's a line from a song attributed to the Roma (gypsies) that says: "The heather will fade and the bracken will die, streams will run cold and clear, and the small birds will be going, and it's then you will be knowing that the terror time has come." We don't have heather here, but the bracken is indeed dying and the small birds, if not gone, have stopped singing. Goldenrod and joe-pye weed and asters rule the meadows and roadsides. It's the temperate middle of August, and already the first fingers of winter stretch into my awareness.

My dilemma with work is less changed than the seasons. I came very close, a week or two ago, to dropping one of the managed care companies that I am a "participating provider" with, deciding at the last minute to stay with it. It's aggravation and constraint on my work versus my ability to earn a living. I'm sure my clients must be in the picture somewhere, but really, these days clients are too often shadowy figures whose needs are only a concern if they are uncooperative about feeling better fast enough.

I met with a woman recently who, emerging from an abusive childhood, has felt for as long as she can remember that she would prefer to disappear. Now she is very ill and may indeed disappear. It's hard to imagine that the two circumstances are not connected. But she is evasive and untrusting, as well as remarkably oppositional. To repair the source of her pain would take years, much of which time would be spent simply allowing her to get used to me, sitting still as she changes the subject and disagrees for the sake of disagreeing, learning gradually that I am not her abusive father. This work is not considered "medically necessary." I can spend a few sessions helping her with her symptoms, with her depression and her unwillingness to eat. Wanting to disappear is not a symptom that responds to brief therapy, and I would be unable to show clear progress. Wanting to disappear may kill her, but that is not the responsibility of her insurance company. This woman is uncertain enough about engaging in therapy that a suggestion that she pay for therapy herself, on a sliding scale, got us nowhere. I suppose that in some sense it was her choice. But the additional economic barrier also was not her choice. For her, the "terror time" has indeed come.

I met last week with colleagues who are planning how to do "utilization review" (a way of evaluating what therapy is necessary and will be paid for by insurance) for a group of therapists of which I am a member. This group is contracting with businesses to offer mental health services; that is, we are ourselves becoming the managed care company. Our clientele is minuscule, but we are starting. As we discussed our vision, it became apparent that our plan is yes, to ask clinicians to describe and justify their work, but then to approve and honor these descriptions if they make sense. That means if they make sense *clinically,* not just economically! So little of my work these days is guided primarily by what's best for the client that I felt elated. Imagine! To decide with the client what is most helpful. To do the best work I can, not just the cheapest work I can! I feel like someone who has been subsisting on TV dinners suddenly asked what she would like to order from the menu.

In a recent movie, *As Good As it Gets,* there is a scene in which a mother describes managed care's depredations of her son's medical care. As she expresses her frustration and rage, audiences in theaters across the country yelled their approval. This is enormously encouraging. Not long ago, managed care was health care's deliverer and golden child. Now, people have become more cynical. I have no doubt that the reforms being discussed in Washington will prove to be no more than window dressing, but a few years ago, no one was even talking about reforms. Well, public opinion may change more slowly than the seasons, and reform that means anything may occur glacially, but at least we are not standing still. Perhaps by the time I am ready to retire I will again be able to practice in a way that is truly healing. Perhaps then the terror time will pass.

Darkness

Gray and a steady rain outside, the kind of day that stirs up loss, a bitter taste like razor blades on the tongue. I've been thinking the unthinkable: that I might drop most or all of the managed care contracts I'm a part of and try to eke out a practice without them. The thought is both compelling and terrifying. I've talked with two colleagues who have done the same, and the news doesn't look good. One said that his caseload is at about two-thirds full; he told me he likes keeping his clinical time limited. Is that true or a rationalization, I wonder? The other also told me that her income and caseload had both dropped by about a third. She now supplements her pay with telemarketing. Can I manage financially with that much of an income drop? Can I manage spiritually otherwise?

I've had two recent encouragements, shall we say. One was a telephone review with a managed care company that is among the most tightfisted. It never allots more than four sessions at a time, and this only after a twenty-five-minute (unpaid, of course) phone session scheduled during free time I don't have. The client in this case was a man with an overwhelming history of recent loss. To top it off, shortly after we started meeting, his wife left him, taking with her their only child. I had met with this client perhaps ten times by the time of the review and the reviewer said that we had to finish meeting within the next four sessions because, after all, this man was functioning and was able to go to work.

Within a week, I got hit with round two, this from a different managed care company. The situation involved a client who had told me that she had an insurance change in July. I noted that I had not yet been paid since the beginning of the year. I'd had a series of go-rounds with the insurance company in my efforts to get paid, something increasingly common, particularly with managed care. When she asked her insurer about this, she was told that, contrary to her understanding, her insurance had switched the beginning of the year, not in July. Because we did not have preauthorization, I would not be paid for that time. Further, I could not ask her for payment for those sessions. Enforced probono work, I suppose.

It does seem as though part of the tactic is to wear clinicians down with errors in payment until we give up trying to get paid, or requirements for authorization until we inevitably make a mistake and are denied authorization. Perhaps I'm being paranoid. Although I have learned from my clients that if you want to understand something about intent, it is wise to look at outcome.

I'm weary of being forced into approaching therapy based on economics instead of healing. I'm tired of the uncertainty and chaos in the field. I'm worn out with being expected to do more: more paperwork, more accounting, more organizing and agonizing and schedule juggling and reading of contracts and keeping track of each insurer's different requirements for less money and less satisfaction.

I have been in a period of my life in which all seems dark and confusing. Part of that—in fact a lot of that—has been this struggle about work. I used to adore my work. I couldn't imagine anything I would rather do or was better suited for. But with the changes in the field I've lost that fire. I still feel engaged with my clients, but my overall feeling in my work is damp, the fire after two days of drizzle.

How I resist change! I wonder whether I should wait it out, perhaps circumstances will change (and I won't have to). I wonder if I'll regret making a change (so perhaps I shouldn't). Maybe I should just wait and see, be sure the decision is the right one (and I don't have to make it now). Ah, how I sympathize with my clients, squirming in whatever ensnares them in their lives. We all, *all,* are frightened and turn our faces from the brightness of the possible. For years I have admired my clients' courage in approaching their futures. But I know it only looks like courage from the outside, that from within it looks like terror and dread and necessity. Well, I have the terror and dread and necessity. Will I allow it to lead me to transformation?

Hedonism Cures Overresponsibility

OCTOBER 31, 1998

Perhaps the ancients considered that the veil between this world and the unseen was thinnest this time of year because the laws of gravity seem so tenuous. The sky, dove gray, steel blue, is soft and cold at the same time. It lowers itself heavily toward earth, as if made of spun lead. The apples, meanwhile, appear weightless: green and russet bubbles floating in the wild trees. Most trees are elegantly nude, but what leaves remain are barely attached, like some leafy cloud caught lightly in the branches.

This is the time of the pagan holiday, co-opted as usual, but still half felt, half seen through its modern trappings of children begging candy and jack-o'-lanterns. I feel the urge to transform myself, in keeping with the season. What shall I become? On Halloween, all is possible.

Several weeks ago I was at a dance party. I don't think of myself as much of a dancer, but that night was different somehow—the right combination of music, more alcohol than usual (not hard to do, since my usual these days is the occasional single drink), and a friendly crowd. I danced for four hours. It was an experience of ecstatic abandon, which, judging from the joy I saw in the faces of the other dancers, was widely shared. I love this kind of non- or loosely partnered dancing. It's mildly sexual, of course, and people danced alone, in groups, and in any kind of couple: women with women, men with men, women with men, all shifting from moment to moment. At a couple of points, communal bottles of tequila (followed by the communal baggie of sliced limes) were passed among the dancers. There wasn't much talking. It was pure group hedonism.

I considered the next day (while nursing my swollen knees and a head fuzzy from staying up until 4:00 a.m.) how few opportunities we have for that kind of release. This can't be good for our collective mental health. Where are our holidays with trance-inducing dance or music or mind-altering substances and people sneaking off into the bushes for illicit sex? We need opportunities to get out of ourselves, out of our precious egos and the steady labor of responsibility.

My clients' lives are much like mine: the job that refuses to stay within reasonable confines (Could it be that our parents had forty-hour workweeks? How quaint), the family obligations, the community tasks demanded of the good citizen who cares about schools or politics or changing the world. All this has been gravely noted; the media has given us statistics and advice. But we have not been advised to blow it off occasionally and seek opportunities for ecstatic abandon. Hedonistic loss of ego is not the recommended solution. Perhaps it should be.

Slipping the Bounds of Self

It snowed yesterday and again today. I can practically feel the earth canting away from the light. Driving home, I could barely make out the mountains, a dream of white layered behind a wash of cloud. Louis Armstrong's voice singing of the "dark sacred night" runs through my mind. Do other people's minds sing commentary on their days, I wonder?

One of the great perks of doing therapy is that one develops a good sense of the range of "normal," but every once in a while there's something such as this that my clients haven't mentioned. Then I'm back in that before-being-a-therapist reality, the one that's limited to what I know just from my own life. Ever since I thought about such things— early adolescence, I suppose—the privacy of the human mind and spirit has struck me as odd. *Wrong,* somehow, sadly wrong. How can something as richly wonderful as a person's inner life be always locked inside? What kind of strange design is that? I felt as though I had mysteriously landed in an unfamiliar country where some essential aspect of experience was unaccountably missing. With time, I've learned how to speak more of my own inner life. With doing this work I've had the opportunity to hear of the inner lives of others.

My motivations to be a therapist are not unlike those of many other therapists I talk with: the desire symbolically to heal one's own family and self, the satisfaction of intimacy safeguarded by therapy's structure, the fulfillment of doing something well and with artistry. But it may be that the opportunity to slip at least partway out of the chafing confinement of the individual human self is an older inducement to me than those.

Becoming Visible

Okay, it's true. So right now she's scared and not in such great shape. She drinks too much and she's gotten herself in trouble with it. She keeps screwing up her life so badly, it's just a matter of luck that she's still working and living in her apartment and not out on the street or in jail or dead. She's too skinny because she doesn't eat well and too broke because she spends impulsively. She chooses the wrong men. I can see all of that; I worry about her.

She also is startlingly honest with me, even when it costs her. She has wisdom, although I don't think she's aware of it, and compassion. She has learned a lot about herself, even if she hasn't figured out how to put it into practice consistently. She may look bad now, but she used to look much, much worse. I have watched the courage it took to get herself this far. When she sits in front of me, I see her possibilities like some kind of ghostly overlay. She's one of those people who could make a difference in the world. She will be powerful and effective when she can allow herself to flourish. I pray her luck holds out long enough.

Her spiritual sister is a woman who was orphaned at three and kicked from relative to relative until she lost track of her self and became instead whatever her companion of the moment wanted. I say "companion" because she has never let anyone close enough to become a lover or even a real friend. Far better to be alone than to risk that kind of loss again. Her life is shapeless, like the clothes she wears, designed to make her invisible. Her life motto might be "offend no one." Our work together has been a bit mysterious to us both, although I have learned to trust it: a series of sudden sorrows and symptoms that appear to come from nowhere. I would no more consider trying to direct it than I would think of trying to sculpt smoke. Besides, how will she find her soul if I am one more person she has to adapt to?

This week I said something to her, I forget what, some comment about what seemed to be going on for her. She responded by saying, no, it wasn't that, it was something a bit different, and she described it to me. Whoo-hoo! Being a trained professional, I sat reasonably in my chair and kept talking with her. But my spirit had hopped up and was dancing around. She said no to me! She articulated her experience and gave herself shape, her own shape! Lately I've noticed that she's been looking more directly at me. I read this as an indication that she's taking form, a sign that increasingly there's someone there to look at me. She's turned some corner, I think, and I am having the same experience with her as I do with the other woman. I see her self, defined and powerful, waiting, just behind her eyes. I can't wait to meet her.

ಬಿ *1999* ಜ

The Truth About Sin

Someone told me a secret today. People tell me secrets every day, of course: about their affairs, or childhood abuse, or panic attacks, or how they really feel about their partners. But this was one of those secrets that defines who you are (if you let it), the kind attached to such a load of shame that the woman telling me had trouble breathing when she tried to say it. She has told no one else, ever. She was sure that I would feel disgusted with her, as disgusted as she feels about herself.

I was raised Catholic. I'm not a Catholic now, but the concept of sin is familiar to me. I wouldn't define sin the way the Church does, but I do believe that sin exists. It exists as intentional separation from the sacred in our connections with one another. We sin when we say something mean and say it to hurt. We sin when we could easily be kind or generous or loving and just don't bother. I don't mean to suggest that we can or should always act from our best selves. I can barely manage to be my okay-self most of the time. We need to allow one another lots of latitude for being tired or having a bad day, for being up against a tendency toward crankiness, for any of our multitude of human limitations. And I'm not talking about the moral choices we make that inevitably are only a matter of "more right" rather than surely right. We mostly do what we can and can't be expected to be ethical giants or models of unending compassion. I mean the everyday choices, the small ones usually, in which choosing the right thing would be just as easy as not. The times we disappoint ourselves. The times when we really could have done better and we know it. It's the spiritual version of shooting yourself in the foot. It feels stupid and unnecessary, and it hurts. That's a sin, and it's worth being ashamed of.

Most people are ashamed about the wrong things, as far as I can tell. I once was walking to my office and was stopped by a boy of perhaps ten who asked if I had a bathroom he could use. I said no and directed him to the public bathroom in City Hall, some two blocks away. I think now of how uncomfortable he must have been to have stopped some woman he didn't know. I think about the small kindness I could have offered by showing him to my office bathroom, which was right there. I was not in a hurry. I did not feel threatened. I knew I could have helped him and it would have been easy. And I just didn't, for no reason. That was a sin, and I still feel a tiny flicker of shame at my selfishness—appropriately, I think. But I do not feel ashamed of the times I was angry because I was pushed beyond my endurance, or the times I could not be loving because I was too hurt to manage it. There is no shame in having been used badly or in being reckless with despair, nothing but sorrow for poor choices made in ignorance or self-hate.

My client was young and alone and desperate. She picked what seemed like the only choice in a context of few resources and less self-respect. I feel deeply sad for the young woman she was and some anger at the life circumstances that led her to feel so friendless. I have respect for her ability to live through what she did and am impressed with the courage it took to tell me about it.

I have heard therapists described as secular clergy, and I made my hearing of this secret a sacred act as far as I was able. I listened with my best self, the self that is profoundly loving. I imagine that most people would agree that what this woman did was wrong, but I would not call it a sin. I see no reason for shame. She owes herself an apology, perhaps. More important, she owes herself love. Until she can manage that, she can borrow mine.

On the Way out the Door

Two weeks now before I go on vacation for the longest time I have taken off in my adult life: three weeks. Here, at least, is one area where managed care has been a boon. Because I am seeing so many people for so much shorter and often more superficial work, my being away isn't nearly as hard on most people as it would have been some years ago. The downside is that I now see many people every other week or on an as-needed basis rather than weekly. And they would all like to have an appointment just before I go and just after I return! Understandable, but impossible.

Mysteriously, too, I've gotten calls from four or five clients whom I haven't seen in months or years, all suddenly now in difficulty and wanting to come in. How did they know I was going away? They didn't, of course; it's just Murphy's Law of Therapist Vacations that made them all show up now. The corollary is that the timing of this vacation will be horrific for at least some clients, and likely more. So far, I have two in that category and a third teetering on the edge. It's tough, that part. These are people whose well-being I care deeply about and whose journey I am committed to. I have backup, of course. But for something as intimate as therapy, backup is really good only for a crisis. But if I waited for a good time to leave, I would never go away. If I always took short vacations (which, in fact, is generally what I do), my spirit and ultimately my work would suffer. I leave gladly. I am looking forward to this time away with great pleasure. But there is always a small ache before I go for what it costs others.

One of the calls from a former client was from a woman I initially saw many years ago, during my first year in practice. "A founding member," she says. I've met with her for a series of sessions a couple of times since our first run, but haven't seen her in a few years now. Her voice on my answering machine started out shaky and then gave way to sobs. She came right to the point. Her three-year-old daughter was dead, killed in a car crash. I felt like I'd been struck by that car as well. How in the world was she surviving?

There's so little anyone can do to help with loss, and that goes for therapists as well as for anyone else. I can be available. I can be un-afraid to talk about it, to listen even to the things that aren't so nice for her to feel, to say. I can keep an eye out for problematic guilt, for any tendency to close down the grief prematurely. If I'm lucky, I can sometimes add perspective here or there in a way that eases the load somewhat. I can make sure she's sleeping, eating. But mostly it comes back to the only thing any of us can do: be there. Stand next to her, physically or emotionally. If her world has just been ripped apart, at least we can hang onto her so she doesn't fall through the rupture. This woman has good friends; she won't fall far, with or without my support. She's actually not one of the people for whom my vacation timing is especially awful. But I'm well aware that when I'm away en-joying myself, she'll be in hell.

The second rule of being a therapist: Learn to live with paradox. (The first rule is, If what you are doing isn't working, try anything else. We're in the change business here!) I am absolutely connected to this woman's torment, as well as to the effect my being away will have on the client whose life is in turmoil right now, on the one who has just learned to trust me, on the person who has been hanging on from week to week. And yet I am just as aware of how many days I have un-til I leave. When I get closer, I will invariably start counting down cli-ent hours. I love them, but I love myself as well. And—hooray!—I'm going on *vacation!* Perhaps the first rule of being a therapist is actually, Attend to your own well-being so that you can care for the well-being of others.

Hard Work

Reentry from this vacation has been remarkably smooth. So far, the only person clearly in worse shape than when I left is the woman whose daughter died. The initial shock and numbness has worn off. But I don't think she would be doing any better if I had been here.

I've returned to find some personal clarity. Funny how leaving your life for a bit makes some things obvious when you see them afresh. I have taken steps to hire someone to do my billing for me. I have always done my own billing, but insurance has become more and more convoluted, and error rates have risen astronomically. As insurance has added more and more "ifs" to payment (sure, we'll pay for therapy . . . *if* you have obtained preauthorization, and *if* you accept a lower rate, and *if* we have recorded the authorization, and *if* . . .), it has added more opportunities for mistakes, and I now spend hours every month following up on claims that are denied in error. It's frustrating, especially since I'm not in a position to stay on hold or wait for a return call. I'm sure that handling phone calls such as mine costs insurers time and money, as it does me. It's hard to see how this system is an improvement. But that's moot, since soon someone else will be doing it for me! It raises my expenses, of course, but it will also raise my well-being. And to my postvacation eyes, it looks plainly worth it.

The other thing I've noticed is how *hard* my job is. When you do something day after day, no matter how complex or difficult it is, you get used to it. I can imagine anyone saying that—a single mother, the secretary of state, a neurosurgeon—"Well, it's my job." But I feel the way that single mother might feel when she's been away from her children for three weeks, has slept well every night, has had time to herself every day, and then returns to the endless needs of a toddler or two. Or the neurosurgeon after a couple of weeks at the summer place reading novels and fishing, coming back to look daily upon death, each person under her or his care experiencing a pivotal health crisis. Therapy demands a level of presence and attention, hour after hour, that is draining as well as rewarding. Actually, "draining," although true enough, is not the point. Lots of jobs are draining. Therapy requires a commitment of the entire self. And sometimes the entire self would prefer not to be involved.

Last night in my writer's group we were talking about laziness. We all avoid writing; it's too much work. What's work, clearly, is not the effort of sitting in front of the computer, or having ideas, or even finding time. What's work is opening the self. As with therapy, it means not settling for the thing you know easily, the ready explanation. As with therapy, it requires staying with the unarticulated, the chaos, the discomfort. It calls for keeping your gaze on your soul even as you squirm and want to get away. It's work to stay fully alive; hard to resist the seduction of coasting, hard to hold steady in the vividness of the fully experienced moment. It's how I would imagine I would tremble under the gaze of the divine: not from fear, and not entirely from effort, but from the weight of awe.

What I've Learned

Now, almost five years later, perhaps I can begin to write about it. Not that I didn't write at all; I poured anguish into my journal, as I did into the kind ears and hearts of my friends, my partner, my family. "Sorrow shared is sorrow halved," goes the saying and, awash in sorrow, I bailed desperately. It seemed as though I never stopped talking about it. But I could not write in this context, could not find the place of my sorrow in my work, except in occasional allusions to it.

My mother's death crushed me. I was seeing an acupuncturist at the time and her diagnosis was, "Your energy system has collapsed." *Yes,* I thought, *my energy system and my heart and my very bones, collapsed from the weight of the loss and the suddenness of it.* Unexpected loss, I have discovered, carries its own special horror. I have understood that horror academically, the "shattered assumptions" of the trauma survivor, and now I knew it personally. For the first couple of weeks afterward, I met the criteria for acute stress response, the official diagnosis for the initial reaction to trauma. For months afterward, I met the criteria for major depressive disorder. The diagnosis book differentiates major depression from bereavement, of course, but they do so by saying that the more serious depressive response to bereavement lasts no more than two months. How was that amount of time chosen? What losses did the writers of those definitions experience in their own lives?

For two months at least I wept daily. I'd never been much of a weeper, and now I made up for lost time. I made a rule: No crying until after work. I've always been astonished at my clients who can do leave-no-trace sobbing. I look a mess for what seems like forever afterward. And I'm not one of those people who feels better after crying; I feel exhausted and in need of a nap, coffee, or both. So I kept myself glued together at work and wept in the car on the way home, in the evening, weekends. It's amazing how much of one's free time it takes to grieve!

I let things go. I took as much time off as I could, allowed my caseload to drop. Grieving was like having a second job. In fact, it *was* my job, more important in many ways than the one that brought in my income. I'm a psychologist. I know well what unmourned loss can look like years later, how it can poison relationships and shut down the heart until you are terrified to find your way back to yourself. I also had the blessing of many years' worth of experience with intense feelings. I know they don't kill you. I had the gift of scores of models in my clients over the years, people who had acted with extraordinary courage and looked the terrible thing in the eye and survived. So, as a friend described, I let it rip.

I wonder sometimes, looking back, what my work was like during that period. With just one or two carefully thought out exceptions, I didn't tell my clients what had happened. Some knew, when I canceled their appointments, that there had been a "family emergency." Others, whose appointments I had already canceled because I had planned to attend a conference that week, did not even know that much. I'd consulted with a colleague about this and decided that mentioning my loss to clients meant taking the focus of therapy away from where it belonged and risked leaving some feeling that they should protect me from their own needs and distress. To those who asked, I responded simply that the family crisis had been settled.

I know there were times, many times, when someone said something that pierced me and I briefly had to break my connection with them and steady my breathing until I felt able to focus empathetically again. I know that a couple of clients (those whose response to trauma included developing a preternatural ability to read people) commented to me after a few weeks that I looked better—implying, of course, that I had not looked so great before. I did what I could to stay present in my work, kept an eye on myself, got consultation. I especially worked hard to make sure I was responsive during those times when a client's pain echoed my own. As far as I can tell, I did all right. And in spite of its demands, work was a relief. In fact, the only times I felt okay, especially in the beginning, were after acupuncture (another mysterious effect of acupuncture) and in the middle of a series of appointments. My clients' stories took precedence over my own for at least a short while.

I have learned a great deal. I know something about what I can bear. I know how little anyone else can do to soften the effects of that kind of pain—mostly just listen, stand by you, and perhaps occasionally cook—and how very important that small contribution is. I've learned that friends who are unafraid of one's tears are precious, and that sometimes one finds understanding in unexpected places.

I know the details of grief's face: the slowing down of time, the hollow wound in the belly or the chest, the feeling of estrangement from humanity, the restless ache, the reverberating finality with which the universe changes. I know that unexpected loss is like no other, and that eventually all loss is the same.

I have become a better therapist, I think. I understand more. My compassion has deepened. I have become a better person as well. There is so much less to fear. I would give it all up in an instant to have my mother back.

Invitation to Joy

MAY 6, 1999

Spring in Vermont is like an illustration for the concept of delight. Imagine: The mornings drenched with birdsong. The young leaves a gathering cloud of green softening the shape of the hills. Wildflowers scattered with careless generosity: trillium, wild oats, trout lilies, spring beauty. Spring beauty! The new cherry leaves are cinnamon red, holding their white blossoms like a gift. In the woods the ferns uncurl, a forest full of questions. Do you notice that subtle expansion in the chest, the sensation of lifting and opening? I feel myself emerging from a long darkness, the bear waking from hibernation, blinking in the saturation of light, hungry and open after long deprivation, greeting the world with its ursine smile.

A client last week told me about something she'd read in a collection of essays. The author had had one of those experiences where a second meaning pops out from behind the obvious one. In this case, it was a simple statement about the rules of some game, but how applicable to the whole of life: *You must be present to win.* This client is someone with a long history of managing the repercussions of her abuse history by dissociating. She has spent most of her life desperately clutching whatever might buffer her from contact with her feelings: the prescription drugs, the overspending, the habitual crises. But I have watched her turn deliberately from that security and toward the impossible, like a woman prying her own fingers from the life raft to set out swimming across the ocean. I have seen terror and determination in her eyes. It had to have taken unbelievable courage, although I am quite sure that she would think that a preposterous assessment.

You must be present to win, she tells me, the woman who has swum through the storm to shore. She's a bit bedraggled still, and coughing up water, but she is focused on the welfare of her spirit nonetheless. *You must be present to win,* I tell myself while walking this morning, having just begun to emerge from my own complicated mix of loss and illness and confusion. *Take in the day; it's glorious.*

Honor

Integrity is linked to power.

I've been mulling over how to be helpful to two clients, both young men. Both have difficulty with drug and alcohol use, minor trouble with the law, mildly problematic risk taking or impulsive choices. What leads someone to choose immediate pleasure even when it costs in the long run? Neither man is thoughtless or impetuous in an uncontrolled way. But they are lost, both of them. Lost boys.

An adult has a sense of honor; his or her word counts for something. A promise, after all, is a currency of the self and the self counts for something. But when the self has no substance, neither does one's word, whether is it a commitment to another or to one's own goals and values. Both of these men can describe what matters to them, what they want for themselves and what they believe in. But their lives are nonetheless without guidance, adrift. They can talk about where they want to go, but they cannot take the helm. It's circular. If you do not steer your life, you never get the satisfaction and sense of power that comes with intention and effort. If you do not choose the honorable thing, even when it sometimes is harder, then the self wilts into ineffectualness. A line in a song says, "I lost my power in this world, 'cause I did not use it."

I have had any number of people confess prior crimes to me, often people who have traveled some immense distance in therapy and look back with shame and sorrow at what felt necessary or inevitable when they were suffering, emotionally unconscious, and simply trying to survive. These are individuals who have worked hard to finally feel strong and capable, but it is clear to me that their personal power will be limited if they do not find a way to hold themselves accountable, to "make amends," as the folks in AA say. It is not enough to feel regret.

If you claim responsibility for the pain you put into the world, you also claim power. You were and are more than just a victim of your own injury at the time. If in addition you right the wrong as much as possible, you give the self weight and significance. You say, in effect, "My choices matter, as do I." My values are important, as am I. I hold myself accountable because I am capable of treating myself and others honorably. And that is my intent.

Starhawk, I think, says something to the effect that keeping one's word is necessary to the successful practice of magic. Therapy is a form of magic, if you consider magic the art of using will to influence transformation (also Starhawk's definition, I believe). From that perspective, honesty with my clients, keeping the implicit promise of the hour and its meaning, is more than professionalism; it is central to my ability to practice my art. If I can live my life consistent with my values, to that extent I will be effective. When I say to a client, "You can do this" or any other incantation designed to create possibility, they do not listen to my words, but to my integrity.

In *Peter Pan,* the Lost Boys needed a mother. They needed the nurturing provided by Wendy in the story. But I think my clients, these lost boys, need something closer to the traditional role of the father. They need to be invited to hold themselves accountable. Expecting something of one's clients is usually a therapy no-no, but these men need to feel that they matter enough—to me and to themselves—to be asked to live honorably. They need to feel not just that they are lovable, but that they are worth being proud of.

Still Miles to Go
Before We Sleep

JULY 15, 1999

I've been meeting with this young woman for a while now, and it's been slow slogging for her. She's one of those people with an easy, outgoing nature, something I (as an introvert) admire. She was always the life of the party—until she was raped. She described feeling carefree, secure in the love of her husband and two small children, secure in her life—until she was raped. She talks now about her life the way traumatized people do, as divided into *before* and *after*. Her life, like her spirit, has been compressed into a fraction of its former size.

No matter how much we talk about it, she still is caught in the idea that she could have avoided the rape, a perception that reduces down to feeling responsible. It's at the heart of all the fears she's developed. If she stays vigilant, she imagines, avoids certain places and activities, is always in control, perhaps she can prevent another assault. She knows better, but that doesn't mean she feels better.

At our last meeting she was talking about the onset of her struggle. It really didn't get to be such a problem, she explained, until the state's attorney chose not to prosecute the case. There wasn't enough evidence, he said. It made her feel as though he didn't believe her. It made her feel that it was her fault.

I suddenly saw the dilemma through the lens of our difference in age. I came of age during the second wave of the women's movement. I *know* that the justice system is biased about virtually everything related to women, including the prosecution of rape. I expect it. This woman is young enough to be my daughter, and she is the daughter of the women's movement. She expects fair treatment. To me, failure to prosecute a rape means that something is wrong with the justice system. To her, failure to prosecute means that something is wrong with her.

I am a little awed that in the space of a generation we have accomplished enough for this woman to believe that gender equity is normal. I am delighted to hear her assume that her husband will cook and clean, at her casual comfort with saying no to sex that doesn't appeal to her. But I am also well aware that mixed in with the influence of feminism is its backlash. The forces of conservatism have taken every opportunity to announce gleefully that feminism is dead, outmoded, and unnecessary. They have had exactly this goal, that the pursuit of social justice be relaxed or dropped. And so this woman has not thought it important to consider her gender as having political implications. She's a sitting duck. When the county prosecutor tells her that she has no case, she feels much the way a woman of my mother's generation might have felt: guilty. Ah, the revolution: three steps forward and two steps back.

The Truth About Relationships

JULY 29, 1999

I read one of those ubiquitous studies about relationships recently. The researcher had asked couples what they thought was most important to a successful relationship. The results were yawningly predictable. Communication, honesty, trust, blah, blah, blah. I found myself a bit mystified by my own annoyance. After all, who can argue with the importance of "good communication"? Isn't trust critical to relational success? You would think a therapist would value these things.

But in a conversation with friends later I found myself saying, "It's all beside the point." Another woman, the intellectual of the group, said, "The discourse in the United States about relationships is very superficial." Both of us are in life partnerships of thirty years' longevity. I am fascinated to find that we agree that honesty and communication are not the secrets to a good relationship, not at all.

Couples often come to my office saying that they need help with communication. It's not that they're wrong, exactly. They know that when they talk they misunderstand each other. They know they get hurt too easily, that somewhere along the line the person whose love brought warmth and delight has somehow begun to tear at the heart. They feel bewildered and angry at the betrayal and hurt beyond bearing. They hope desperately that I can see what damage their partner is causing and persuade that person to return to loving them. In couples therapy, I can depend on having a starting perspective so dramatically different from that of my clients that it's a wonder we can talk at all.

Learning to make a relationship work is a form of spiritual development. And as with all spiritual development, the task seems improbable, the mind gets lazy, the psyche digs in its heels. A sustained relationship requires a form of radical acceptance: acceptance of the truth of the other, and that their truth is not yours. "Of course, of course," I can imagine my impatient reader thinking. "Yes, yes, I know she's a separate person," says my client. Ah, but do you? We all secretly want the good mother in our relationships, the one who responds fully, who knows what we want almost before we know it ourselves. Radical acceptance means not only knowing that the other person may not meet your needs. It also means welcoming the difference in vision that leaves those wishes unmet.

Loving really does have to be openhanded. You love because you do and because you choose to. You love as a discipline and because the act of loving enriches you. You love as the choice of a deeply independent person, responsible for yourself, expecting nothing, and all that you get back is a blessing.

I rarely meet that standard myself, of course. I get cranky and judgmental. I am sure I would be much happier if only my partner would change in this or that way, in short, be more like me. Luckily, relational success, like parenting success, depends not on perfection but only on a good heart, a reasonable effort, and the continuing choice to return to a loving stance. Trust, like the miracle of being known by another human being for thirty years, is a by-product.

The Lesson Repeated

It was a couple of days into my vacation. I was paddling the canoe midmorning and began to notice flashes of light in my visual field. I knew this was a symptom to take seriously and called the optometrist. By late afternoon I was in surgery with a retinal specialist, having tears in my retina spot-welded with laser. How I Spent My Summer Vacation.

The timing, in fact, couldn't have been better. It's not easy for me to leave work in the middle of the day. Under the pressure of a series of appointments, I may have been tempted to wait and see. Acting immediately probably saved my vision. I had the luxury of several unscheduled days in which to recuperate. By the time I returned to work, any remaining damage was visible (as changes in vision) only to me.

But more than odd visual effects are visible to me. This event means that I am vulnerable to a recurrence and to retinal detachment in both that eye and the other. I now live with the knowledge that losing my vision is a real possibility. This experience has pushed me farther along the path that my mother's unexpected death opened up. Life looks less and less the way it did several years ago. My assumptions are different, and assumptions create reality.

Therapy is a great way to distill clarity from the muddy swamp of discomfort. It can turn around how you feel about yourself and your life. It can offer skills for managing the challenges of anxiety or depression. Therapy is a way to find possibilities where you thought none existed, and comfort when ease felt beyond hope. But therapy does not change the terms of life, which include pain as a given. Perspective can make a difference in how the pain sits in one's heart, but no amount of understanding or acceptance can change the fact of the pain or the necessity of living with it.

I am reminded of the woman whose child died. We met a couple of days ago. For her, therapy is not a matter of learning skills or sifting through confusion or changing perspective; her pain is simple and direct. I have only my company to offer, but I know she feels helped by that, by being with someone who gets it, someone she does not have to protect. What she does not know is that I also feel helped by her. I cannot compare my experience to hers, of course. Losing a child is perhaps the gold standard of anguish. But in the last several years, I have had enough familiarity with the abrupt tilting of my world to feel that I live with the same existential knowing that she does. Not many of us live here, and it is good to sit together occasionally.

Presume nothing, says the voice of the universe. Do not take your health for granted, or your faculties, or the well-being of anyone you love. What you hope for has no bearing on the movements of fate. Prepare for the journey, but know that the path is unpredictable and much of it beyond the touch of your wishes or plans. Know this and stay open anyway, for joy also comes unmediated by your intentions.

Choice

SEPTEMBER 15, 1999

In graduate school, I recall learning the importance of reflecting feelings at the same intensity with which the client expressed them, a kind of precision in mirroring. But often there is value in altering that intensity. For someone who is overwhelmed, recognizing the pain while describing it as just a notch easier can make it possible for him or her to experience the distress as slightly more manageable. And even more often, people look sideways at their pain, underreport it, accuse themselves of playing up the problem, when all the while I am looking beyond their words at the unacknowledged shadow, years of ache behind the small portion that they're describing.

So it is, too, with naming the nature of the task. Some people, it's true, come for help with something fairly circumscribed: learning to manage stress or depression, getting support while traversing a difficult divorce. But for many the task may look limited but its meaning is not. For them, how we describe what they are doing makes all the difference. Words shape actuality, and when heroic work is called such, a person feels the relief that comes with recognition and finds the stamina that comes from honoring the size of the struggle. We've all heard stories of heroism; *Reader's Digest* is full of them: ordinary people who did something impossibly brave because it had to be done and because they knew it mattered. My office is the *Reader's Digest* of the spirit—ordinary people doing the extraordinary.

I think of the woman who lives with what might classically be described as a mental illness. She has been in the hospital many times, sometimes under grueling conditions. And each time, she has done whatever she could to retain and succor her spirit, and done so even though her mind was reeling out of control and her body was being assaulted with treatments that destroy as well as help. Her choices under those circumstances have been heroic, and I have told her so. Appreciating the true extent of her valor may help hold her up the next time she is slammed by her illness. For her, there will always be a next time. I watch her with admiration.

Or there is the man whose family and experience has taught him that his life means nothing, less than nothing. Every day he is faced with dozens of choice points, moments in which he will act as if his future counts for something or will let go into despair. It must feel like those times backpacking when you are beyond exhaustion, not able even to hope for the goal, taking each step only because you know that you are committed to continuing. He faces each of those moments alone. But in his hour a week with me, we can at least call the journey what it truly is: a battle for the soul. And courage often is displayed not in pulling the child from the burning building, but in the small choices unnoticed by others.

So often change comes down to this. There is an existential moment, the moment of decision, when all the therapy in the world cannot alter the fact that you must actually do the difficult thing. Therapy can make the choice visible (some might say tormentingly visible!) and can offer a kind of symbolic companionship. But in the end it's a matter of personal courage. You feel the pull of all that's familiar and secure, and you turn deliberately toward the unknown door of possibility. You do so repeatedly in spite of what it costs you. You elect change over and over, as a kind of spiritual practice, because the welfare of your soul is indeed at stake.

Acceptance

Our first frost was last night, late this year. This morning I walked accompanied by the soft clatter of frost-hardened leaves slipping to the ground, enchanted rain. The sunrise is like tropical fruit—mango, papaya—and for a while the sky and the trees seem to exchange light, the air suffused with color. Robins, so noisily territorial in the spring, are gathering quietly in groups, preparing for the journey. I miss them already. The season demands acceptance of change; I resist.

I met yesterday with the woman who was raped. She has been mourning her old self, the young person who loved to go on adventures with her kids, who met life with her face open and full of laughter. "If you look at pictures from before, you wouldn't even know it was me. I don't look like the same person," she tells me. As she talks, I remember looking at myself in the mirror after my mother died. I recall again my astonishment in seeing that I still had a face, recognizably human, familiar. I felt so profoundly changed that it would have been less of a shock to have discovered that my features had rearranged themselves, that I had acquired fur or pointy ears.

Nancy Venable Raine, in her book about her recovery from rape, talks about her friends living "in the Great Before, a place I could never return to." The woman talking with me wants her "before self" back. When she looks in the mirror, she compares the image to who she was, and is horrified at the change. Our experiences start with the similarity of shock and then diverge dramatically. My change, after all, was the product of love. To be changed by losing my mother felt painfully right. Of course I would turn toward it. Her change was the product of hate. No wonder she turns away.

Yet she can no more return to her old self than we can demand summer back by resisting autumn. The seasons, at least, transition gradually. Life also is supposed to ease us from stage to stage. Childhood fades, we mysteriously find ourselves with jobs and apartments, middle age sneaks up on us. The horror of trauma is partly in its abruptness. We find ourselves reeling from the shock, bewildered and frightened and unprepared. How did I arrive here? I don't understand how anything works in this foreign place. I want to go home!

When she talks of wanting herself back, what she really means is that she wants to reverse time, to undo history. But it's *her* history, evil as it is, and to refuse it is to refuse herself. I am reminded of another client, a woman whose first forty years were crushed by childhood emotional and sexual abuse and its aftermath. She is angry sometimes and weary of the struggle and would not wish her life on anyone, least of all herself. Yet she says that she would not wish to have had a different life, because her history has created who she is. Valuing yourself ultimately means making peace with your history. And I will enjoy winter only if I can allow the robins to leave.

Taking Stock

It's after the peak of foliage; the red leaves and the tourists, ephemera both, have drifted away. Each nice day now feels like a bonus, a prize in the cereal box. The hillsides have that tweedy look, a rich orange-gold, curry and marigolds, mixed with evergreen and the soft gray-brown of tree limbs that is exactly the color of deer. In July we take the weather for granted, but now when the wind can easily carry a cold rain or even flurries, everyone remarks with gladness on the occasional reprise of summer. I spent the day happily outdoors, putting the garden to bed, planting bulbs, rebuilding part of a rock wall, starting the process of hunkering down for winter. Tonight is the local church's chicken pie supper, the seasonal marker for midfall. It's enormously satisfying to live in a place where the earth's turning still shapes one's life. We may not celebrate Samhain, but we have the chicken pie supper.

I turned fifty this fall. The last several years have been marked by loss in my personal life and turmoil in my profession. Managed care continues to dictate the practice of psychotherapy. I have a client now, a woman with lifelong difficulties in relationships, including with herself, whose insurance company has assured her that she has "unlimited benefits" for therapy. They have assured me that they will pay for "acute stabilization" only. The dilemma in a nutshell. My solution so far has been to inform clients as much as possible about the realities of insurance reimbursement and to collaborate with them about how to proceed. That way I avoid the worst trap, that of trying to force-fit the client's agenda into that of the insurer. I am still being pulled in two directions at once, but at least I have company. And it's a way to keep the *client,* rather than the insurance industry, as my employer. It's not much, but I can tell I'm on the right track because of the responses I get from insurers. (You want the *client* to participate in his or her case review for authorizing more sessions?! What is your clinical justification for that? You had better be doing this on *your own* time!)

Loss is less easily solved. Reliable health and the lives of those closest to me were something I had always presumed, like the ease of July days. My life now is like this day, October sixteenth, a lovely day even more cherished because two days ago there was snow on the ground. I suppose I could say that I have come to something like acceptance, but the term is too flat for the actuality. The actuality includes struggle, because acceptance has an annoying habit of refusing to sit still. And it includes gratitude.

In the eye that was damaged, I can still see visual changes that tell me it is not fully healed. And so I am always a little worried, conscious that all is not well, monitoring for further injury. But mostly I am aware of the glorious gift of vision, which is not a given in life, the ability to see the sunlight shimmering on the leaves, liquid gold and copper against the sky. I'll go to the chicken pie supper tonight and laugh with my friends. And if you hear a resonance in my laughter, a kind of depth and release that was not there before, it's because of the abandon that comes from tears.

Authenticity

I've seen this man off and on over many years; he settles into the session comfortably. We both know his psyche with the easy familiarity you feel in a house you have lived in for years. He does not dissemble or sugarcoat his observations of himself. He has long passed the time for such artifice with me. I bring myself to the meetings as much as I can in the spirit of perfect service and presence. I have long since passed the time for needing to collect information with him.

I don't recall the precipitant, if indeed there even was one. But I experienced in the session a few moments of absolute transparency. Amazing, even more so because of the barrier of our different genders. But we were for that time no more than two souls, simply *there*. I felt that if we met in an afterlife we would recognize each other. I have no idea if that moment was mutual—probably not—but I am sure that the nature of the relationship that made it possible is shared.

Peter Kramer, in *Moments of Engagement,* says that

> It is characteristic, it seems to me, of good dynamic therapy that, despite all concealment, the patient comes to know the therapist with great immediacy. Is the therapist trustworthy or secretly cruel, confident or anxious, loving or withholding, generous or self-absorbed, sick or well? The analysis is very much with one specific person.

Regardless of what the textbooks and the graduate programs and the workshops may imply, you cannot separate the technique from the person. And I would advise anyone to choose a therapist based on character and heart before method and knowledge. Although it has been my observation that experience often offers a rough gauge of the former. Perhaps people don't stay in the field if they don't have the character for it. Perhaps that kind of attention over many years and with many people develops heart.

I do more and more "technotherapy" now, of course: helping people develop skills to manage anxiety or to self-soothe or to think differently about their problems. It's the best you can do in a few sessions with managed care wanting "specific goals in behavioral terms." I'm more actively focused on "fixing" things; I have to be. But the time that I spend with people who have the luxury of unraveling the deeper layers of their pain, the therapy of the heart, is my form of meditation.

I've never had much luck with regular meditation. It always feels kind of pointless to me. But the meditation of service, ah, that's a different matter. Empty the self: quiet the ego-driven voice that cares about how I look to others or is endlessly trying to accomplish something, to get something for myself. Be still. Open the heart, bring the mind's entire attention. Paradoxically, in letting go of personality I feel most truly myself. It reminds me of holding my little nephew as an infant. In his gaze he was fully there, a complete soul before the shaping of family or culture or the terrible necessity of personal wounding. He had temperament but not personality; no wonder infants seem so wise.

I often feel relatively transparent in session, although not often as completely so as I did in this session recently. Do you remember that movie in which the aliens were simply made of light, and had fashioned a human skin to wear so as not to seem out of place when they visited? Perhaps that's my goal: to become only light with skin on. Another several lifetimes of being a therapist and I might get there.

৪ৃ 2000 ৫৪

Coming to Terms

JANUARY 1, 2000

Here it is, a new year/century/millennium. I've reached an uneasy balance with my work, one that I am adjusting continuously in response to the ever-changing insurance picture. I resigned from the worst of the managed care panels, the one that required phone reviews and would authorize no more than six sessions at a time. It's caused hardly a ripple in my practice. I only had a few clients with this insurance, and I gave them all plenty of notice. A coalition of therapists that I belong to has captured one of the primary local contracts, and we are continuing to review cases based on what is best for the client rather than solely on economic efficiency. We have already been challenged about this (Why should they buy our "product" when they can get it cheaper from the competitor?) and are under increasing pressure to operate more like the other managed care companies. It remains to be seen whether employers are willing to pay more to get more.

I have stopped accepting new clients with the most difficult of the managed care insurances, the one with the lowest pay and the worst paperwork, the one with the philosophy of care that says "We don't pay for problems in living" (a direct quote), the one with the scary fat contract that protects them and puts me in untenable positions. The newest wrinkle is that they are beginning to audit the therapists who work with them. This audit means that they send you a list of perhaps 150 minutiae (I swear I am not exaggerating), covering everything from the detailed information that they want in your case notes to how your office is equipped, then visit your office and look through your files to make sure that you're living up to their standards. It's not that I disagree with most of their standards, although I do disagree with some, such as requiring every therapist in private practice to be on call twenty-four hours a day, seven days a week. I disagree with the obsessive level of information that they believe I should collect about every client. Most of all, I disagree with this level of intrusion, not so much into my office as into my practice, into my relationships with actual people, who, by the way, signed away any privacy rights to their insurers.

In the past I've talked myself into working with this company by saying that I wanted to be available to people who had this insurance, which means a substantial number of people in my area. Do I give up that availability because I don't want somebody snooping through my clients' records and telling me to carry a beeper? On the other hand, how much intrusion is too much? I am reminded of the (supposedly true) description of cooking a frog: If you drop a frog into boiling water, it will do everything it can to get out of the pot. If you put a frog into warm water and gradually turn up the heat, the frog will cook without ever struggling.

Choosing not to work with managed care leaves me feeling like some relic from the past, someone unable to change with the times, holding on to some outdated romantic notion of what I think therapy should be. Staying with managed care makes me feel like a sellout, someone who has bought the mythology that less is better and that form is everything. No, it's not just that. It means acquiescing to the notion that the insurer, not the client, is my employer. That's the bottom line. The insurer tells me what problems count as worthwhile, what information I need to ask for, what kind of therapy to do with someone. They tell me how to arrange my practice and my records as well, but that is secondary. My alarm at the audit is symbolic; it's not that I'm so concerned about someone examining my office or my records. It's that I'm concerned about this level of muscle flexing and what it represents: we are agreeing that my practice is their property in some basic way. The conflict is about control. Do these therapies belong to me and to my clients or do they belong to the company which pays the bills?

Another partial solution has been to do what I can to encourage people to pay for their therapy themselves. Obviously, for some people, it's impossible to pay at anything approaching a reasonable fee, which is why we have insurance . . . except that so often insurance isn't working anymore for "mental health" problems. But discounting my fee substantially has brought it within range of at least some people, which gives them the option of doing the therapy they feel they want and need, rather than the therapy their insurer deems "medically necessary." It's not that my regular fee is unusually high. I charge somewhat less than what the insurance industry considers "usual and customary" for this part of the country, which is low by any urban standard. But the major managed care companies have cut their costs by significantly cutting what they pay me, and if I'm willing to accept this from them, why not accept it from those who pay out of their pockets? So now more than a third of the people I see are paying for their therapy themselves, because they don't have insurance, or they don't want managed care prying into their therapy, or they want the kind of therapy that their managed care companies don't want to pay for.

The whole situation is a little like a garment that doesn't quite fit: if I roll the sleeves up and undo the button where it's tight and wear a jacket to hide the stain, it sort of works. It's nothing like comfortable, mind you, but it's manageable for now.

This hardly feels like a long-term solution. I am acutely aware of offering two standards of service, one to those with unmanaged insurance or who can pay for themselves, another to those with managed care. The insurance managed by my colleagues falls somewhere between the two, but closer to the better service. It's not fair, but it's today's reality.

I think more about leaving the field. I think about semiretirement, about accepting only clients who do not have insurance restrictions. In the meantime, I notice that I am taking substantially more vacation time, probably six or seven weeks this year. Most insurances have dropped the fee that they will allow me to collect. (How I'd like to do this in my own life! I could say to the grocery clerk. "I see that my total comes to $67.83, but I'll pay you $52.50." To the electric company: "I'll be sending you $27.30 instead of the $45.72 on this bill.") More vacation isn't helping matters in the income department, but my income if I stopped working would be drastically lower! I have read in professional newsletters that my colleagues who are keeping their incomes level are doing so by working significantly more hours, seeing thirty-five or more clients a week. I am unwilling to do that. I already work longer by virtue of the added paperwork, and I am certain that more client hours means poorer therapy. Managed care has already compromised my standards. If I cannot keep the satisfaction of work with integrity, I might as well take another job, any job. I draw the line here.

The Existential Moment

Every once in a while, someone gets to one of those major life choice points. I don't mean this in the usual way: the job, the relationship, the baby. I mean it emotionally: authenticity or disguise? Connection or isolation? Which will it be? Remember, your life is at stake.

Don't get me wrong, I'm well aware that we make those choices daily, hourly. But think of your own life. Weren't there times when the stakes seemed higher, much higher? Weren't there times when you could intuit that your decision did more than shape the moment before you, it shaped your future in some inexplicable way? Often, making the choice feels like a matter of breathtaking courage, a leap into the unknown. And, oddly, those moments often are not particularly visible to others; they're not those kinds of choices. Will you really say how you feel, say it perhaps for the first time? Will you take the risk, do the thing that you have never done? These are the big ones, the decisions that change one's life course. They are the times when you can almost, but not quite, and certainly not without cost, see some new way of being in the world open before you. Sometime later you may have another opportunity, but to decline the possibility in the present diminishes you in some subtle way, and you know it. It's terrifying.

It makes me think of a man I see whose whole life is focused on his job. He has a long commute and a responsible position where he is expected to work long hours. He has a family, a partner and a young son; he rarely sees them. He knows that he's drowning, that's why he's in my office. And he feels impossibly caught. He can't begin to imagine a way to work fewer hours in his profession, let alone in his current work setting. More deeply, he can't begin to conceive of a more intimate relationship with his family. After all, this is the frightening possibility that his work prevents. And underneath that, how could he dare to live without the armor of his job? Who would he be? How would he trust that he had something to offer, something worth the love and attention of the people that matter to him? We've just started together. He is well aware of the first layer of his dilemma but has not described the others. I'm guessing at them. But I can predict that he will face a moment when he has to choose, when he has the first intimate conversation with his partner or when he first elects to leave work at 5:00. It won't be easy. (Special reader bonus points: Figure out how to describe the work he needs to do in behavioral terms. Make a plan for how to accomplish this in fewer than eight sessions.)

With someone else, the critical moment is now, well into her work with me. Painstakingly, she has laid the foundation: a life that is stable, free of alcohol and drugs, with a steady job and a collection of acquaintances. She has learned that she might, just might, be worth more than she thought, more than the assumptions that she had based her life upon, more than the assumptions she learned from the parents who ignored her. Now she has to decide: Will she act as if she really matters? Will she tell someone the truth about how she feels (sad, always sad) and ask for support and, hardest of all, accept it? Will she reach for closeness for the first time in her life? I can describe the scene. She is having lunch with someone she works with, perhaps; her heart is pounding and she can barely get the words out. This person will see that she seems anxious, or may notice that talking so personally is a bit different for her. But the colleague will not know that this woman has just rewritten the future that her parents bequeathed to her, that her life is now irrevocably different.

Sometimes people hang out in that almost-ready state, hoping that with more therapy they will somehow get more comfortable, hoping that the choice will get easy or that it will happen by itself. Occasionally it does, but usually not. The thing sits before you, but you have to put out your hand, trembling, and invite it forward. You have to commit yourself to the change. It is a deliberate act. I can help someone prepare, but I cannot do it for her or even with her. Like death, it is always faced alone. I walk with her to the threshold, stop, and open my hands as she steps forward.

Forgiveness

Years ago in a college art class we were assigned the task of making a valentine card without using any red. Interesting how changing that one central association allowed something else to emerge. The past couple of days we've had warm-temperature snow, the kind that coats every twig. It sits thickly on the pines, blurring their detail into great white waterfalls. Snow climbs up every tree, an extravagance of snow, each limb and stem a mere underline for its luxuriance. The bending branches make every road a tunnel. The landscape is voluptuous with snow, its lushness like that of a jungle, if you can separate the notion of jungle from that of green.

So much of the task of therapy hinges on disentangling elements that are presented as inseparable. I met recently with a young woman who, though smart and capable, was failing in college. Her mother pushed her, she said, frantic for her to do well in school. Predictably, the more her mother demanded, the less the daughter produced. She was sacrificing her own future on the altar of her emerging independence, and she knew it, but couldn't help herself. "You're in college; you don't have to show Mom a report card anymore," I said. "So lie. Get good grades, for yourself, and tell your mother you barely passed." As I'd guessed, the possibility was enough. She started doing well in school and decided to tell Mom the truth after all. What she really needed was to feel grown-up enough to be in control of what she told her mother.

Or consider the notion of forgiveness. The topic is in the air enough lately that people sometimes come in with it as an agenda. And well they should. I think of a woman who is emotionally exhausted. If she could forgive her ex-husband, forgive him his alcoholism and the affair he had that ended their marriage, then perhaps her days wouldn't be consumed with imagining how she could show him, could finally explain conclusively, just how badly he hurt her. I remember the man who is restless, who wonders how he can ever let go of his anger toward the priest who touched him sexually long ago when he was in grade school. If he could let it go, he says, maybe he could manage to go back to church. Maybe then he would find some peace.

The trouble is that "letting it go" feels dangerously close to "letting him off the hook." It's the idea of forgiveness as blessing that people can't stand, that sense of wiping the slate clean, of thereby giving something to the person who hurt you. This is especially true when the offender has not been brought to account in any way, has not sought forgiveness or even recognized an injury. In that case, the injured person is the only one who continues to hold the truth of what was done. That, at least, is a kind of justice. If no other kind is forthcoming, then how could a person possibly abdicate? It would be irresponsible.

The leap here is separating out the elements of accountability. One who has hurt another is responsible for that damage. But it is not the duty of the individual who was hurt to personally bring the offender to justice. The truth of the transgression does not go away or lose its gravity when the person harmed recovers. Evil is an account that will be called due: by karma, or the Wiccan's "Threefold Law," by the grinding discomfort of the guilty conscience, or by some form of the final accounting envisioned by so many religions. Harm we do to another harms us: ask anyone in AA, where making amends is central to recovery. We cannot get away with anything. Our transgressions, like our kindnesses, shape our psyches and our futures.

But the reality of forgiving someone is another matter and often requires a sideways approach, as with that college student deciding to lie about her grades. I recall my own efforts, over a decade ago, to relax an angry stance toward someone who had hurt me, one of those life-defining betrayals. I just couldn't swallow that "he did the best he could" pap. That's exactly the point, isn't it? That someone was self-centered, or angry, or greedy? Wrong isn't when you do the best you can and fail. Wrong is when you don't bother, when you choose your own feelings and needs over someone else's pain and elect to ignore the consequences. Face it: we've all done it, even if only in small ways.

I couldn't let it go, so I did an about-face and decided to hang on. *I will* never *forgive him,* I announced formally to myself. And then, as time went by, the constellation of my experience changed. My anger seemed less interesting; my injury, although no less important, felt less relevant to my current life. I still like the idea of the person who hurt me "getting it" about what he did, but I really don't feel like it's my job to see to it that he does. I just don't think about it much.

I think that's forgiveness. If this man came to me now and asked, I'd say "Sure, I forgive you," meaning: You owe something, but not to me beyond having asked. Figure out for yourself how to pay your debt. To myself I might think: A woman who can see the jungle in a snowfall should have no trouble looking past the limitations of her history.

What to Do When You
Don't Like It

It's been an odd winter: virtually no snow until late January, and then almost four feet in less than a month. Mud season promises to be a doozy, given all that time for the cold to penetrate the ground without insulating snow. With the sudden snow cover, my mailbox became just a mysterious door embedded in a snowbank at the end of the driveway. Open it if you dare. The three or four steps leading to the front door transformed into a kind of snow ramp, handicapped access for mice. Two days ago the weather abruptly turned milder and now the snow thickens and condenses, snow fleas miraculously appear from nowhere, and I spot the first downy edges of pussy willows on the bush that I know from experience tends to bloom early.

Some people are not very likable when I first meet them: the man who is self-absorbed, the woman who complains endlessly about how people take advantage of her. I have a friend who is a wiseass and would invariably ask me about work by inquiring after "the whiners." Sometimes, sitting with one person or another, I would think she was right. It's easy to understand how this man finds himself virtually friendless, how this woman has had a series of failed relationships.

There's a saying in Vermont that "If you don't like the weather, wait a minute." So too, I have learned with my clients to wait and see, not to take my initial feelings all that seriously, especially feelings of annoyance or of being put off. It's only the person's presentation, like a coat, and if I notice without becoming attached or reactive, if I can hold who they seem to be loosely enough, then they may unfold enough to show who they actually are. Interestingly, I always, without exception, feel warmly toward the reality of the person. I'm no longer even surprised when someone who felt hard to take settles in comfortably next to my heart. Oh, I like some people better than others; that's natural enough, the unfortunate secret of the parent. But not to like someone at all means that we have failed together. I have failed to stay easy and open about who that individual might be, have failed to offer an invitation to authenticity that she or he could accept. The client has failed to meet me, to risk showing more than how she or he has learned to manage the challenges and terrors of intimacy.

I wish I carried the lesson into my personal life more. You'd think I would have learned, but I find it far too easy to decide in haste that this one is a bore, that one not worth my time. Like spring's promise, right under the snow, I know for a fact that if I could give it time and care, each person I pull away from is someone I could like. Although in "real life," of course, I don't have permission to invite them out of themselves. I don't, in fact, have the heart; it takes such heart to hold someone in a loving gaze without his or her cooperation.

There's an old joke: "Everyone talks about the weather, but no one does anything about it." It's like that with people; each person's nature is a given, as unassailable as climate. But therapy is sometimes an astonishment, the circle within which the laws of nature and relationship no longer apply, where a lifetime of winter softens into hope.

Midlife

I like being middle-aged. It's so much more relaxed than young adulthood. Having had fifty years to get used to my flaws, I just can't get so worked up about trying to look better than I am. I like the complexity of perspective it affords. The lesson of middle age is that perfection, like simplicity, is an illusion. A client about my age noted wryly that it was getting harder to tell the good guys from the bad guys. The bad guys, after all, had some redeeming, even appealing, qualities and the good guys, it turns out, were sometimes a pain in the butt.

I don't like the body hassles very much, of course. My car is seven years old and we seem to be about the same age (car years must be similar to dog years, about seven to the human year). It's mostly reliable, but I have to put up with a few little annoyances, such as having to guess at the gas level because the gauge doesn't work. It squeaks and rattles, as do I. The finish doesn't look like it used to; the miles show. But what the hell. I like a face with a few miles on it.

Walking yesterday morning, the snow on my neighbor's pasture was a perfect sweep of white. Maybe that's what's so fascinating about snow—that flawlessness, so unlike what appeals to me in people. For a few minutes at sunrise, its white expanse was washed with a glaze of color so transparent that perhaps, after all, it existed in my mind only.

Omnipotence

MAY 14, 2000

If you do it right, therapy is terribly dangerous to the person of the therapist. I don't mean the burden of empathy, although that will cost you your youth, regardless of the age of your body. I don't even mean the risk of practicing a certain odd combination of intimacy and perspective in relationships, although that does tend to lead the unwary into the twin perils of intrusiveness or distance with the people we love.

It's been said that people cannot *not* communicate. Silence has a thousand shades of meaning; even breathing signals feeling and intention. I can read anger, hope, alliance, resignation, anxiety, despair, and release in breath. I think most people can do the same, conscious or not. Mostly we dip into the top few layers of communication; that's enough, even plenty, to make understanding possible. What happens, though, when the whole of your attention is focused on understanding? When you have arranged the setting and rules of the interaction so that little interferes with that connection? What if, more than that, you have practiced the discipline of relaxing the usual ties to the self and its concerns, practiced being available to the stream of communication from the other? It is not so surprising to imagine that you might, in fact, sometimes get information in nonordinary ways. Or, to be more accurate, you might sometimes get information in ways that are not ordinarily used. That's when it gets dangerous.

It's a form of power, that intuition. Sometimes I can simply feel the accuracy, sometimes the client tells me: the example I choose that just happens to refer to some reality in the person's life, the leap to a particular connection that is unpredictably helpful, the surprise insight about what something means. I still respond with a little shock, except that it has become so familiar that it's hardly shocking. Sometimes clients say, "How did you know that?" I say, "You told me," and it's true. Not with words, perhaps, and maybe not even nonverbally (whatever that means), but I assume that if I have the information, it's because it was shared with me.

Okay, so where's the danger, you wonder. That small feeling of surprise signals the danger, the client's asking about it signals the danger. No person gets responded to so completely in life that she or he lacks all hunger for recognition; no person is so secure in life that she or he feels no need at all for power. We are all, to one degree or another, frightened and insecure in a world of imperfect relationships and unpredictable futures. If intuitive knowledge is a form of power, then like all power that feeling is invariably seductive. It's seductive to feel special. It speaks to that in all of us which feels small.

There are antidotes—luckily, or we would all be corrupted beyond endurance. Perhaps the most important is compassion for the client. Power used in the service of compassion is harmless. If what matters is the client, not the self, then all will be well. Sounds easy, doesn't it? And certainly, feeling for and with the client is not hard. But *only* feeling for and with the client is what's difficult. Ignoring the temptation to enjoy just a bit of the attention for myself, even if only in the privacy of my mind, takes intention and will.

Another antidote is understanding the nature of my own vulnerability to being seduced by power. If I can admit to its appeal and smile with compassion at the foolish self who wants the impossible reassurance of omnipotence, then it's not so hard to let it go and step back into the mud with my fellows. Besides, we can only pretend to live elsewhere. The solution to how tempting it is to feel special is to be common as dirt. Sometimes a client will urge me to accept credit for having done something amazing. Sure, I'll take credit for being skilled and having a good heart. Anything amazing belongs elsewhere, out there in the universe of human possibility, perhaps, or in the realm of the spiritual. If you grab at it, it dissolves. Take my advice: Stay common as dirt and allow the winds of the divine to blow through you.

Searching for the Truth

People preserve them carefully, these secrets. Everyone imagines that pain is hard to find, deeply buried, perhaps not even recalled. In fact, we each, like the god of Adam, construct our lives and relationships from our own ribs and blood and breath. What else have we to build with? The real truth, the thing that matters, is woven seamlessly into our daily lives. The best hiding place, after all, is right out in the open, where you would never think to look.

I'm not talking about symptoms here; it's easy to agree on symptoms. And I don't mean the kind of symptoms so dear to the hearts of managed care case reviewers, difficulties such as phobias or obsessions, which often have little to do with the complexities of one's injuries to the spirit and more to do with the vicissitudes of biochemistry or learning. These are not the people who come to me saying, "Help me with this problem." They arrive saying, "Help me with my life." Getting information is never the challenge. People tell me everything I need to know clearly and repeatedly. The challenge is that neither of us knows at first what is really being said, what it really means.

Do you remember those "magic eye" pictures that were popular a few years back? Each had a pattern that looked random, but if you looked at it with your eyes just a bit unfocused, if you looked *through* it, another picture popped into view. It was there all the time, hidden in plain view, right in the pattern.

I am reminded of a woman who cannot stop eating. You would never know it, if you saw her. Her metabolism's quick and she vomits up the rest. She grew up with a series of stepmothers after her biological mother died. Her father, a charming alcoholic, flitted from wife to wife, each younger than the other, women barely out of girlhood themselves and in no way prepared to nurture another girl. Deeply unnourished, she fed herself in an act of defiance—plenty of food, more food than you could ever need. If her parents wouldn't take care of her, well, she would more than make up for it. She couldn't mother herself, but at least she could feed herself. She did well in school and, later, in work. Everything looked fine. Everything except for the girl who was still eating furiously.

This woman is a child therapist, but she had never listened with compassion to the story of that girl. In a way, she is responding to her own history the way that her stepmothers responded to her as a child: by turning away. Partly it had never occurred to her to do otherwise; after all, she knows her history, why dwell on it? Ah, but there's a difference between knowing what happened and opening your heart to the lived reality of what it meant for a child of six to lose her mother; for her to be unable to turn to her surviving parent for comfort or even basic care; for her to hope for love from a second mother, and a third, only to face more loss; or for her to feel alone in the world and alone with a sadness too big for her to comprehend. Here, of course, lies the other reason for this woman's seeming indifference to her own history. If she listens with her heart, she will feel what she suffered. And she still has that old instinct from childhood, when she knew intuitively that if she really felt it, she would be crushed. Now, of course, she is a grown-up. She has more resources. Moreover, she has already survived. She can afford to turn toward that girl instead of away.

She tells me the pieces: her never-satisfied craving for food, her history of raising herself. She describes a constant, low-level discomfort, an equal mixture of tears and rage, that no amount of eating seems to soothe. And I imagine a girl of only six years being faced with a loss she can't begin to digest. I imagine her despair and growing rage as the alleged adults in her life continue to fail her. That feeling gradually shapes itself into a single bold move that both rescues herself and holds them accountable. She will make a life that works well enough, but she will not forget. Her caretakers' culpability piles up with every bite she takes.

We all carry such secrets, of course, if not always so dramatically. No one gets to adulthood without some hidden insecurity, some sense of limitation, a half-understood anxiety or sorrow. Mostly we manage them as we do our small bodily infirmities. One person gets frequent headaches, but finds that aspirin generally does the trick; another can avoid those heartburn flare-ups by not eating spicy food. No one expects perfect health; we're happy enough to get occasional relief. But oh, imagine the joy of a girl of six, released from the terrible isolation of the secret she has carried forever, her message understood at last.

The Other Path

OCTOBER 1, 2000

Sometimes the most therapeutic thing is to stop going to therapy. I remember a woman I knew years ago who had been in therapy for most of her adult life. She wasn't sure she could make it without therapy. She'd always had someone she could depend on to guide her through life's shoals. With her therapist to catch her, she knew she could never fall too far. But she also never felt completely adult. How could she? Further, she was living a self-definition as an injured person, someone always in need of a bit more support than others. For some people, of course, allowing themselves to check in with a therapist is one form of self-love. It can be a way finally to relax into support for those who have spent much of their lives unsupported and alone. For this woman, however, therapy had become part of how she knew she was never really all right, a proclamation to herself that she would always be damaged. One of the most helpful things we did together was to agree that she could and should leave.

Another client has spent many months twisting in indecision, miserable in her job but unable to leave it. Indeed, she has been unhappy with her career choice almost since she entered her field some twenty years ago. She has made a number of changes about ways to make the job a slightly better fit, but not the change that really matters: to change careers. The rest of her life is similar: she modifies this, does better with that, but the bottom line is that her life continues to be out of balance. This woman is forty-six years old and is aware that she is not immortal. She is wasting her life, and she suffers from it. Yet there is some bottom-line way in which she still fails to claim ownership of her life, and coming to therapy is part of that. As long as she is talking with me, as long as she is making incremental changes, she is not faced fully with the existential challenge of responsibility for herself. And so we agree to stop meeting, at least until she feels some clear inner shift. She can avail herself of my counsel and help with preparation, but when it comes to the central task, she must face it alone. Anything else is self-deception. I left her with some final reminders: that one can feel afraid and still act, that the nature of the deepest task is often that it feels like the very thing one cannot do. We said good-bye.

A third client is experiencing what I might call a crisis of will. He is anxious, has panic attacks. He has cooperated (with a prior therapist) with all the standard treatments for these difficulties, with only minor relief. This is not surprising. I have watched him comply with the letter but not the spirit of his therapy homework. But more deeply than that, he is scared of what real healing would mean. It would mean re-thinking his marriage of fifteen years. It would mean challenging the unwritten contract of that relationship, which requires that he be too preoccupied with his distress to insist that his wife be faithful to him. More fundamentally, it would mean deciding that he deserves to feel better. I cannot decide that for him. This one is complicated by that fact that his insurance is managed care. There was a time when I might have kept someone such as this company as he looked for the resolve to put his heart into what he must do. Now we cannot afford that. I don't know if that is better or worse for him. Perhaps the necessity of finding such resolve without the reassurance of my presence will sharpen the outlines of the choice for him. Or perhaps the lack of any reminders about what he's trying to do will mean that he loses his resolve, gets distracted by his everyday life, and feels like a failure. I hope that he can hold onto a sense of purpose. He has to want his life, his well-being, more than he wants the comfort of the familiar. I will be here when he chooses.

ᘒ CONCLUSION ᘓ

Counting My Blessings

Over thirty years ago, I started working as a therapist. This means I've been doing therapy for virtually all of my adult life; it's how I've spent a sizable percentage of my waking hours. I've worked with literally hundreds of people, some for just a few sessions, some for years. Hundreds of lives: a thousand secrets; ten thousand moments of intimacy, of shared anguish, laughter, and the tender surprise of transformation.

Doing therapy changes a person. This should not come as news, I suppose, except that I have rarely heard others mention it. Any job done at length affects a person by the simple expedient of practice. The lawyer becomes more analytical and perhaps argumentative; the professor, didactic. I, as with other therapists, I assume, have gotten more intuitive, with an impulse to help which can become intrusive if I'm not careful. And I'm clearly more skilled at intimacy than I used to be. After all, I've been in training, so to speak, for a couple of decades. I feel at home with closeness. I understand how to create it. As a side effect of one's job, this seems to me enormously more useful than, say, skill at computer repair or office management.

When I was a child my father delivered newspapers as a second job. I sometimes went with him and quickly came to notice newspaper boxes wherever I went. Now, years later, they're no longer salient, and I don't "see" them anymore. I'm sure that the clothing designer sees the cut of a garment, whether he or she is working or not, in a way that I never notice. Even when "off duty," I see human distress, recognize who's depressed, notice how people treat one another.

What's more compelling, however, are not the changes that can be attributed to habit and practice, but those that are instead a consequence of knowing. By this I mean the knowing that comes with a particular kind of lived experience, that in-the-bones knowing that changes the substance of who you are. I am reminded of the Adam and Eve story in the Bible: once you eat of the tree of the knowledge of good and evil, your life is changed utterly. What follows is a description of some of those changes.

Only in the past few years has there been some writing about vicarious traumatization, the secondary trauma experienced by the helping person who bears witness to the stories of others' abuse. Although I don't consider myself vicariously traumatized, I do know that I have not been immune to hearing other people describe their pain. I am acutely sensitized to the reality of how people inflict hurt on others, to how relationships are a medium through which the damage one person bears is passed to another, most often parent to child. Most parents do better with their children than anyone who truly knows them would expect, but it seems virtually impossible not to bequeath at least a residue of hurt and confusion to the child. And pain is transmitted as well between partners, co-workers, friends.

In the telling, that pain is also passed to me. I'm well protected, of course, by the nature of my relationship with my clients. But I have learned a great deal about cruelty, intentional or not; about heartbreaking loss that can never be fully comforted; about the fundamental sorrow of life and the essential careless inhumanness of human beings. I rarely watch movies or television shows that could be characterized as drama. They just feel like more work, and I am weighted down by the drama already present in my life. I watch sitcoms. They're resolved in half an hour and I may even get a chuckle. I garden, which is a way of reinforcing hope. I sense that my capacity to contain and attest to suffering is unnaturally enlarged. I know that this costs me in some way, but I don't yet fully know how. I imagine my heart in my chest worn down like a stair tread walked on for generations.

But doing therapy is also like watching spring come every year for several lifetimes. Just as inevitably, person after person opens into herself or himself, comes unlocked from the cramping confinement of history and habit, shines with clarity and power. I have watched innumerable acts of courage, and have learned that when it counts the most, my integrity and emotional reliability matter far more than any skill or technique I can contribute. It is equally obvious to me that although my participation is usually helpful and occasionally crucial to what happens, the magic that occurs in therapy is by no means the creation of the therapist. In the end, the possibility and direction of the change belong to the other person.

I do not mean in any way to undervalue what I, or other therapists, do. After all, if the person were able to get untangled himself or herself, it is unlikely he or she would have arrived at my door. I am quite aware of my role as alchemist, daily handling the power to transmute. Nonetheless, there is an organic process at work here, some impulse toward completion and well-being, that is the real agent of transformation.

How can I witness miracles and not be affected? In my own life, I have the great fortune thus to know how to assist my own transformation. I trust unequivocally the human capacity for resolution, regardless of how dark the way appears. When my mother died suddenly a few years ago, I had no reason to fear my sometimes excruciating grief. I knew absolutely that the psyche has the capacity to heal even what feels impossibly destroyed. I have watched with humbled amazement as people—many people, not just the rare exception—did what I knew to be the hardest work of their lives. And so I know that if humans can be limited and self-absorbed, they are also unarguably brave and loving and full of honor. The work of therapy is spiritual work, in that it rides on the wings of the ineffable. That lifts me as well.

Intimate acquaintance with so many lives offers a window on the multitude of ways that people live, both practically and psychologically. People are endlessly inventive, and one of the benefits of being a therapist is that you don't have to live locked in the limitations of your own perspective. For myself, this has meant a kind of compassionate softening, a recognition that there are many solutions to the dilemma of being alive and that "human nature" is as various as human appearance. I am privileged to have some sense of the range of what is normal, in the sense of workable as well as frequent. That knowledge is comforting. Being a therapist tends to create tolerance, and it's a small step from there to self-acceptance.

And so, most important is the change that comes, unexpected, as a summary of all these elements. If therapists are exposed to what is most tragic in life, we are also privy to what is most inspiring. We have the benefit of experiencing many lives. If we are paying any attention at all, we have the possibility of developing wisdom.

Now you, the reader, have looked through the window of this journal into the experience of being a therapist, as well as into my own life. I imagine that you have seen yourself and others you know reflected in these pieces, that you have variously agreed and argued with me, had your own thoughts and feelings in response. If my work has offered me the opportunity to learn wisdom and compassion, my wish is that through these essays I may pass some of that gift along to you.

Order a copy of this book with this form or online at:
http://www.haworthpress.com/store/product.asp?sku=5084

DIARY OF A COUNTRY THERAPIST

_____in hardbound at $29.95 (ISBN: 0-7890-2115-3)

_____in softbound at $19.95 (ISBN: 0-7890-2116-1)

Or order online and use special offer code HEC25 in the shopping cart.

COST OF BOOKS_____

POSTAGE & HANDLING_____
(US: $4.00 for first book & $1.50
for each additional book)
(Outside US: $5.00 for first book
& $2.00 for each additional book)

SUBTOTAL_____

IN CANADA: ADD 7% GST_____

STATE TAX_____
(NY, OH, MN, CA, IIL, N, & SD residents,
add appropriate local sales tax)

FINAL TOTAL_____
(If paying in Canadian funds,
convert using the current
exchange rate, UNESCO
coupons welcome)

☐ **BILL ME LATER:** (Bill-me option is good on
US/Canada/Mexico orders only; not good to
jobbers, wholesalers, or subscription agencies.)

☐ Check here if billing address is different from
shipping address and attach purchase order and
billing address information.

Signature_____

☐ **PAYMENT ENCLOSED: $**_____

☐ **PLEASE CHARGE TO MY CREDIT CARD.**

☐ Visa ☐ MasterCard ☐ AmEx ☐ Discover
☐ Diner's Club ☐ Eurocard ☐ JCB

Account #_____

Exp. Date_____

Signature_____

Prices in US dollars and subject to change without notice.

NAME_____

INSTITUTION_____

ADDRESS_____

CITY_____

STATE/ZIP_____

COUNTRY_____ COUNTY (NY residents only)_____

TEL_____ FAX_____

E-MAIL_____

May we use your e-mail address for confirmations and other types of information? ☐ Yes ☐ No
We appreciate receiving your e-mail address and fax number. Haworth would like to e-mail or fax special
discount offers to you, as a preferred customer. **We will never share, rent, or exchange your e-mail address
or fax number.** We regard such actions as an invasion of your privacy.

Order From Your Local Bookstore or Directly From
The Haworth Press, Inc.
10 Alice Street, Binghamton, New York 13904-1580 • USA
TELEPHONE: 1-800-HAWORTH (1-800-429-6784) / Outside US/Canada: (607) 722-5857
FAX: 1-800-895-0582 / Outside US/Canada: (607) 771-0012
E-mailto: orders@haworthpress.com

For orders outside US and Canada, you may wish to order through your local
sales representative, distributor, or bookseller.
For information, see http://haworthpress.com/distributors

(Discounts are available for individual orders in US and Canada only, not booksellers/distributors.)
PLEASE PHOTOCOPY THIS FORM FOR YOUR PERSONAL USE.
http://www.HaworthPress.com   BOF04